Bobby at Home

Fearless Flavors
from My Kitchen

Bobby at Home

Bobby Flay

with Stephanie Banyas
and Sally Jackson

**Clarkson Potter/
Publishers**
New York

I dedicate this book to my mother, Dorothy Flay. For the first eighteen years of my life, every one of my meals at home came from her kitchen. I will miss her lamb chops with mint jelly from a jar and her pork chops with applesauce and a pinch of cinnamon. Each page is filled with the spirit of her memory and a lust for life that only she could attain. Miss you, Mom. xo

Contents

Introduction

As I compiled the recipes for this book, it quickly occurred to me that this is certainly my most important one to date. Not just because it's my newest, but because it's my most passionate. I've had the pleasure of bringing many facets of my life to the pages of my previous cookbooks, telling stories of my individual restaurants and the life that I've lived in them and through them. A handful of volumes displayed my love of outdoor cooking by working my grills overtime and bringing to life every piece of meat, fish, and vegetable imaginable with a spice rub, a sweet and spicy glaze of some sort, and, of course, the perfect char. There were flavors of the Southwest, the Mediterranean, and even a book focused on the greatest American meal of all time: *Burgers, Fries & Shakes.* In contrast to some of the higher-calorie dishes you found in *Burgers, Bobby Flay Fit* brought me and my readers full circle because just as my flavors need to be well balanced (from spicy to sweet to sour and more), so does our overall lifestyle. Hence, *Fit* was a book about how a person who spends both his personal and professional life constantly around food can stay somewhat in shape and healthy.

That brings us to the present. *Bobby at Home* is exactly what it says. It's a collection of my favorite dishes that my friends and family eat when they're in my home. I'm often asked by people what I do to relax when I'm *not* working. Interestingly, and somewhat surprising to most, the answer is: I cook. It's a very different approach than my restaurant kitchen life or when I'm being challenged on TV by what seems like anyone who's ever turned on a stove anywhere in America. At home, it's a pace that's steady but focused, and where the food is always abundant and served family-style.

This book is so important to me because the dishes that grace these pages have real emotion attached to them. They have been accompanied with laughs and tears. Each has a story—and not just that the fried chicken is soaked in buttermilk. These dishes are cooked and shared with my most trusted friends and family, as well as people whom I want to share an important conversation with. I love the idea of getting to know someone new over a bowl of shrimp and grits or doing business with a platter of crispy soft-shell crabs in front of us.

Cooking to me is much more than a profession. It's the way I show my love, respect, and appreciation for the people in my life. If you're in my circle, an invitation to my apartment in New York City comes often. It could be a Kentucky Derby lunch or a Belmont Stakes breakfast. A last-minute call to indulge in a bowl of homemade pasta Bolognese to watch the Golden Globes or an all-day Super Bowl party replete with game-day snacks like Brussels sprouts nachos. Sundays in my apartment are filled with the aromas of brunch dishes like pumpkin pancakes and glazed bacon, and at night, dinner can easily be a spread of chicken parmesan and a red chile Caesar salad. Don't even get me started with Thanksgiving. It's an epic day of classics on lots of twists, football, and late afternoon naps.

My house in the Hamptons is irresistible in the fall and winter, when I cook all-day braises of green pork chili and the occasional autumn "harvest weekend" that includes dishes like brick chicken with salsa verde and gingerbread and lemon curd trifle. But all summer long is when that kitchen really gets a workout. At least once a week, usually on Saturdays, lunch is served at exactly 1:30 p.m. I fill my outdoor wooden farmhouse table with an abundance of summer dishes mostly made with fruits, vegetables, and herbs from the farm stand near my home and fresh seafood from the fishmonger just ten minutes away. The pergola that presides over the table

shades us and the food from the blazing sun. There is never fewer than a dozen guests and usually more like twenty-five hungry people in their bathing suits with a glass of rosé glued to their hands. You'll find dishes like Mediterranean mezze platters, Korean BBQ chicken, and cast-iron porterhouse steaks being passed around the table. I call it lunch because it starts in the afternoon, but to be fair, it's an all-day event. We sit at the table for hours, eating, drinking, solving the problems of the world, and dwelling on the trials and tribulations of our lives. We swim, play bocce, and listen to music with the perfect beat until the sounds of evening tell us another day has come and gone.

Sitting around these tables and breaking bread binds us all together just a little more each time. It's the one thing I look forward to most. It takes thought and it takes effort, but I wouldn't have it any other way. My intention is to help you, as readers and cooks, get the people you care about around your table more often. Don't just think of these dishes as a means to feed someone, but as a way to gather the people in your life you want to spend quality time with. The dishes on these pages all have a language of their own. I hope they bring as much joy to your table as they do to mine.

Welcome to my home. I'm so happy you're here.

Bobby's Essential Pantry and Equipment

Pantry

I think we all know by now that a properly stocked pantry is an incredibly freeing thing—keep a few essentials on hand, and you'll be ready to make loads of exciting dishes on the fly. Here are the staples that I always have in my pantry and the basic ingredients you'll need to make the recipes in this book. Any recipe-related follow-up trips to the market will be easy-peasy: you'll only need the fresh stuff—veggies, herbs, and protein.

Oils and Vinegars
Extra-virgin olive oil
Canola oil
Blended oil (half canola oil
    and half extra-virgin
    olive oil)
Cider vinegar
Red wine vinegar
White wine vinegar
Aged sherry vinegar
Balsamic vinegar

Spices
Kosher salt
Fine sea salt
Whole black peppercorns
Whole dried chiles, such
    as ancho, New Mexico,
    and pasilla
Pure chile powders, such as
    ancho, New Mexico, and
    chile de árbol
Sweet smoked paprika and
    sweet paprika
Ground cumin
Ground coriander
Ground cinnamon
Allspice
Whole nutmeg

Canned Goods
Whole plum tomatoes
Crushed tomatoes
Tomato paste
Chickpeas
Black beans
Hominy
Pumpkin purée (not pumpkin
    pie mix)

Sweeteners
Pure cane sugar
Light and dark brown sugar
Pure maple syrup (dark
    amber)
Clover honey
Molasses
Sorghum syrup

For Baking
All-purpose flour
Fine cornmeal
Stone-ground cornmeal
Baking powder
Baking soda
Pure vanilla extract
Cornstarch

Specialty Items
Pomegranate molasses
Harissa
Gochujang
Saffron threads
Toasted sesame oil
Low-sodium soy sauce
Mirin
Best-quality potato chips
Best-quality tortilla chips
Capers
Cornichons
Anchovies, packed in oil
Canned chipotle chiles in
    adobo sauce

Condiments
Hellmann's mayonnaise
Ketchup
Dijon mustard
Whole-grain mustard
Crème fraîche
Greek yogurt (2 percent and
    full fat)

Equipment

I realize that not everyone's home kitchen is as well equipped as mine—I have been cooking professionally for over forty years, and collecting the tools of my trade for almost as long! There are a few key items, though, that I reach for constantly. They are the pieces that I believe every home kitchen should have, and I have listed those below. It may look like a lot, but chances are you already have many, if not most, of the equipment here. Fill your drawers with these items, and you will find making these recipes all the more enjoyable and your life in the kitchen that much easier.

Pots and Pans
Enamel-coated cast-iron
    Dutch oven
Cast-iron pan
Nonstick pan
12-quart stockpot
3-quart saucepan
4-quart saucepan
Stainless-steel sauté pan

Utensils
8- or 10-inch chef's knife
Serrated knife
Paring knife
Honing steel
Heatproof rubber spatulas
    (small, medium, and large)
Slotted metal fish spatula
Heavy-duty metal spatula
Wooden spoons
Slotted spoons
Flat whisk
Balloon whisk
Kitchen tongs
Microplane
Box grater
Cutlery

Specialty Items
Wooden cutting boards
Plastic cutting boards
Large platters
Large bowls
Mandoline
Digital scale
Deep-fry thermometer
Instant-read thermometer
Pressure cooker
Cazuelas

Small Appliances
Food processor
Blender
Spice grinder
Immersion blender
Stand mixer
Waffle iron

Baking Equipment
Rimmed baking sheets
8- and 9-inch baking pans,
    square and round
9 x 13-inch baking dish
Ramekins
Parchment paper
Silicone baking mat
Glass liquid measuring cups
Dry measuring cups

BREAKFAST + BRUNCH

If you're familiar with me and my cooking at all, then you know how much I love breakfast and brunch foods. I created a show centered around this favorite meal of mine and have written a cookbook on it, too. What's not to love? Fluffy pancakes, crisp waffles, flaky biscuits, perfectly cooked eggs—from sweet to savory and back again, the list goes on and on. I also like entertaining for brunch, which is as much an event as it is a meal. It's the perfect time to break out large, family-style platters and great big pitchers of cocktails, and gather everyone around to indulge as you blur the line between morning and afternoon.

My Favorite Black Pepper Biscuits

Sure, I've included this recipe in other books, but there was no way I could leave it out of my cookbook on how I cook at home! I literally make these biscuits at least once a week, either for breakfast, brunch, or dinner—these biscuits *are* home.

Makes 12 biscuits

4 cups **all-purpose flour**

4 teaspoons **baking powder**

1 teaspoon **baking soda**

1 teaspoon **kosher salt**

¾ cup (1½ sticks) cold **unsalted butter**, cut into small pieces

1½ cups very cold **buttermilk**, shaken

½ cup **heavy cream**

2 teaspoons **freshly ground black pepper** (not ground super fine or coarse—somewhere in between)

1. Position a rack in the center of the oven and preheat the oven to 450°F. Line a baking sheet with parchment paper.

2. Combine the flour, baking powder, baking soda, and salt in a large bowl and mix well. Cut in the butter using your fingers or a pastry cutter until the mixture resembles coarse meal. Add the buttermilk and gently mix until the mixture just begins to come together.

3. Scrape the dough onto a lightly floured counter. Pat the dough into a 12-inch square or round, about 1 inch thick. Cut the dough into 12 equal squares or rounds. Put the biscuits 2 inches apart on the prepared baking sheet. Brush the tops with the cream and sprinkle with the pepper.

4. Bake the biscuits for 12 to 15 minutes, until lightly golden brown. Transfer to a wire rack and let cool a few minutes before serving warm.

Cornmeal-Chive Biscuits
(page 17)

**My Favorite Black
Pepper Biscuits**

Cornmeal-Chive Biscuits

I can't be the only one torn between a flaky biscuit and a wedge of golden cornbread in the breadbasket. With this cornmeal-biscuit hybrid, you'll never have to choose again. It has a nice, tender crumb as well as a touch of crunch and sweetness from the cornmeal. The biscuits are wonderful savory as is, but if you're in a sweet mode, omit the chives and serve them slathered with your favorite jam. You can't go wrong either way.

Makes 12 biscuits

3 cups **all-purpose flour**

½ cup plus 2 tablespoons fine **yellow cornmeal**

¼ cup **sugar**

1 tablespoon plus 1 teaspoon **baking powder**

1½ teaspoons **baking soda**

1¼ teaspoons **kosher salt**

¾ cup (1½ sticks) cold **unsalted butter**, cut into small pieces

1⅔ cups very cold **buttermilk**, shaken

¼ cup finely chopped fresh **chives**

1. Position a rack in the center of the oven and preheat the oven to 400°F. Line a baking sheet with parchment paper.

2. Combine the flour, cornmeal, sugar, baking powder, baking soda, and salt in a large bowl. Cut in the butter using your fingers or a pastry cutter until the mixture resembles coarse meal. Add the buttermilk and chives and gently mix until the mixture just begins to come together.

3. Scrape the dough onto a lightly floured counter. Pat the dough into a 12-inch square, about 1 inch thick. Cut the dough into 12 equal squares. Put the biscuits on the prepared baking sheet.

4. Bake the biscuits for 12 to 15 minutes, until lightly golden brown. Transfer to a wire rack and let cool a few minutes before serving warm.

Master Muffin Mix

This master muffin formula is a brunch basic and a great recipe to keep in your back pocket. Plain and simple as is, a few easy additions will tilt the recipe savory or sweet depending upon your craving. Feeling savory? Try folding cheese, garlic, and/or herbs into the batter. Sweet muffins more your speed? Chocolate chunks or fruit will do the trick nicely. Just a note: Try not to get too overzealous when stirring in those last elements. Muffin batters, like pancake and waffle batters, are best when not overmixed.

Makes 12 muffins

Nonstick cooking spray

2 cups **all-purpose flour**

¼ cup **granulated sugar**
(1 tablespoon for savory muffins)

¼ cup packed **light brown sugar**
(for sweet muffins only)

¼ teaspoon **fine sea salt**

1 tablespoon **baking powder**

1 large **egg**

1 cup **buttermilk**

2 tablespoons **unsalted butter**,
melted and cooled

2 tablespoons **canola oil**

1 teaspoon **pure vanilla extract**
(for sweet muffins only)

Flavorings of your choice
(right)

1. Preheat the oven to 350°F. Spray a 12-cup muffin tin or paper liners with nonstick spray.

2. Combine the flour, sugars, salt, and baking powder in a large bowl. Whisk the egg in a medium bowl until smooth, then add the buttermilk, melted butter, oil, and vanilla and whisk until smooth.

3. Add the wet ingredients to the dry ingredients and mix until the batter just comes together. Fold in your desired flavorings. Evenly divide the batter among the prepared muffin cups, filling each three-quarters full.

4. Bake until a toothpick inserted into the center of a muffin comes out with a few moist crumbs attached, 18 to 20 minutes. Let cool in the pan on a rack for 10 minutes. Remove from the tin and let cool 5 minutes longer. Muffins will keep, tightly covered, for up to 2 days.

Flavorings

Chocolate Chip ¾ cup mini semisweet chocolate chips

Lemon-Blueberry 1 cup fresh or frozen (not thawed) blueberries and 1 teaspoon finely grated lemon zest

Mixed Berry 1 cup mixed fresh or frozen (not thawed) berries

Cinnamon-Sugar Mix together ¼ cup sugar and 1 teaspoon ground cinnamon in a small bowl. Fill the prepared muffin cups with the batter and sprinkle the top of each with 1 teaspoon of the cinnamon-sugar.

Savory Choose one or a combination: ¾ cup grated sharp cheddar or Gruyère cheese, ⅓ cup sliced green onions or ¼ cup finely diced green chiles, and/or ¼ cup finely chopped herbs (cilantro, parsley, chives)

Dutch, Dutch Apple Baby I'm not shy about handing out credit where credit is due, and in this case, hats off to the crew at *America's Test Kitchen* for taking the German pancake to new heights! Dutch baby, German pancake—I don't care what you call it, as long as you try it. This baked pancake's dramatic presentation (it soars like a full-pan popover, high sides surrounding a custardy center akin to a thick crepe) belies how simple its batter is to prepare. And the technique update discovered by test-kitchen royalty? Skip preheating the pan and start everything off in a cold oven. It may take a bit more time to cook this way, but they are totally worth the wait.

Serves 4

4 tablespoons (½ stick) **unsalted butter**, softened

3 large **eggs**

½ cup **all-purpose flour**

½ cup **whole milk**

1 tablespoon **sugar**

1 teaspoon finely grated **lemon zest**

Pinch of freshly grated **nutmeg**

Apple Cider Sauce (recipe follows), for serving

1. Melt the butter in a 9-inch cast-iron skillet over medium heat. While the butter is melting, make the batter.

2. Whisk together the eggs, flour, milk, sugar, lemon zest, and nutmeg in a medium bowl until smooth. Let rest for 5 minutes. Pour the batter into the pan with the melted butter and place the pan in the oven. Heat the oven to 375°F.

3. Bake, without opening the oven, until golden brown and puffed, about 20 minutes. Remove from the oven, slice into four wedges, and serve drizzled with the apple cider sauce.

Apple Cider Sauce

Makes about 2 cups

3 tablespoons **light brown sugar**

2 tablespoons **unsalted butter**, cut into pieces

2 **Gala apples**, peeled, cored, and sliced ¼ inch thick

2 cups **unfiltered apple cider**

¼ teaspoon **ground cinnamon**

Pinch of **kosher salt**

2 teaspoons **cider vinegar**

1. Combine the brown sugar and butter in a large sauté pan and cook over high heat, stirring a few times, until both have melted, about 2 minutes.

2. Add the apples, cover the pan, and cook, stirring a few times, until soft, about 10 minutes. Remove the lid and cook until the liquid has evaporated and the apples begin to caramelize, about 5 minutes.

3. Add the apple cider and cook over high heat until reduced by half, about 8 minutes. Add the cinnamon, salt, and vinegar and cook for 1 minute more. Let cool slightly before serving.

Greek Yogurt and Ricotta with Fresh Fruit

This is one of those breakfast/brunch dishes that looks super impressive but could not be easier to make. Gotta love that when you're entertaining! I'm a Greek yogurt devotee—I use it in my cooking all the time and have it for breakfast nearly every day. Ricotta cheese also has a featured spot in my refrigerator—a dollop of the fresh cheese is a favorite way to finish a bowl of pasta, and it lends itself just as well to sweet preparations, either baked in a dessert or simply dressed with toasted pistachios and a drizzle of honey. You can mix the yogurt and ricotta base together the night before, which lets the flavors really meld and saves you time in the always-busy morning.

Serves 4

2 cups **2% Greek yogurt**

2 cups **fresh ricotta** or best-quality grocery store brand

Finely grated **zest of 1 orange**

2 tablespoons fresh **orange juice**

1 **vanilla bean**, split lengthwise and seeds scraped out

Fresh fruit (berries and/or sliced ripe peaches, nectarines, or plums)

1 cup **prepared granola**

1. Whisk together the yogurt, ricotta, orange zest, orange juice, and vanilla bean seeds in a large bowl. Cover and refrigerate overnight or for at least 1 hour before serving to allow the flavors to meld.

2. Transfer to a shallow serving bowl. Top with fresh fruit, sprinkle with the granola, and serve.

Mrs. Pie's Cinnamon Bread

Mrs. Pie is my assistant and cowriter Sally Jackson's mother. When we learned that Sally's childhood nickname was Salpie, it was game over—we've been affectionately calling Sally "Salpie" ever since, and her mother became "Mrs. Pie" soon thereafter. This soft white loaf with its central swirl of sweet cinnamon is one of Mrs. Pie's prized recipes, the freshly baked loaves a highly anticipated gift to many lucky friends and neighbors over the years. But for as many loaves went out the door, just as many stayed—it's been an all-time favorite of Sally and her siblings for as long as they can remember. Even better, the simply delicious, slightly yeasty bread, with its gooey cinnamon swirl, is now enjoyed by the next generation: Sally's kids love it just as much—if not more—than she ever did. It's the kind of well-loved recipe that every family should have.

Makes 2 loaves

1 (¼-ounce) package **rapid-rise yeast** (2¼ teaspoons)

1½ cups **sugar**

1½ tablespoons **ground cinnamon**

2 cups **whole milk**

¾ cup (1½ sticks) **unsalted butter**, softened, plus more for greasing

2 teaspoons **kosher salt**

1 teaspoon **ground cardamom**

2 large **eggs**

5 to 7 cups **all-purpose flour**

1. Combine the yeast and ¼ cup water in a small bowl and let sit at room temperature until it proofs and begins to bubble, about 5 minutes. Combine ¾ cup of the sugar and the cinnamon in a small bowl and set aside.

2. Bring the milk to a simmer in a small saucepan over low heat. Add the remaining ¾ cup sugar and ½ cup (1 stick) of the butter and whisk until the sugar has dissolved and the butter has melted, about 2 minutes. Whisk in the salt and cardamom, remove from the heat, and transfer the mixture to a large bowl. Let cool for 5 minutes.

3. Add the eggs and whisk until combined. Whisk in the yeast mixture and 3 cups of the flour and mix with a wooden spoon until a soft dough forms, adding more of the flour as needed. Transfer to a lightly floured surface and knead the dough for 5 to 10 minutes, until smooth.

4. Place the dough in a lightly buttered bowl and turn to coat. Cover the bowl with plastic wrap and let the dough rise in a warm place until doubled in size, about 1 hour. Gently punch down the dough, cover the bowl, and let rise again until doubled in size, about 45 minutes.

5. Preheat the oven to 365°F. Lightly butter two 9-inch loaf pans.

6. Divide the dough in half. Keep one half covered with a clean dish towel. Roll the other half into a 15 × 7-inch rectangle. Spread 2 tablespoons of the butter over the surface of the bread, leaving a 1-inch border. Sprinkle half the cinnamon-sugar evenly over the dough. Starting at one shorter end, roll up the dough tightly. Seal the edges tightly by pinching them and transfer the dough to one of the prepared loaf pans. Repeat with the remaining dough.

7. Bake until the loaves are golden brown and sound hollow when you knock on their tops, about 30 minutes. Remove from the oven, brush the tops of the loaves with the remaining 2 tablespoons butter, and let cool in the pans on a wire rack for 10 minutes. Remove the loaves from the pans and let cool on the rack for 10 minutes more before serving. The bread will keep at room temperature, tightly wrapped in foil, for up to 3 days. It tastes great toasted, too.

Challah French Toast with Peach-Raspberry Compote and Maple Mascarpone

French toast has been on my breakfast table forever, but the version I grew up with—squishy white sandwich bread soaked in custard, sprinkled with cinnamon, fried in butter, and drowned in that mysterious "pancake syrup"—well, let's just say that French toast has come a long way, baby! The days of Wonder bread are far behind me, and now that I'm the one in charge of breakfast, my French toast starts with thick slices of eggy challah bread. Maple syrup (please make sure it's real) is always good, but a freshly made topping of peaches and raspberries (or any berries) is *great*. Come fall or winter, I love making apple or pear compote instead, saving the summer fruit for when they're in season.

Serves 4

½ cup **mascarpone**

2 tablespoons **pure maple syrup**

3 large **eggs**

3 large **egg yolks**

3 tablespoons **sugar**

1 teaspoon **kosher salt**

¼ teaspoon **ground cinnamon** (optional)

2 cups **half-and-half**

2 teaspoons **pure vanilla extract**

8 (1-inch-thick) slices **day-old challah bread** (see Tip)

¼ cup **canola oil**

4 tablespoons (½ stick) **unsalted butter**, cut into tablespoons

Peach-Raspberry Compote (recipe follows), for serving

TIP Up to 1 day and at least 4 hours before making the French toast, put the sliced bread on a wire rack and let it sit on your counter to help dry it out.

1. Whisk together the mascarpone and maple syrup in a small bowl; set aside.

2. Whisk together the eggs, egg yolks, sugar, salt, and cinnamon in a large bowl until combined. Whisk in the half-and-half and vanilla and whisk until smooth. Transfer the custard to a large baking dish. Add 4 slices of the bread and let soak on one side for 4 minutes. Turn the bread over and let soak for 4 minutes more.

3. Three minutes before the bread is done soaking, combine 2 tablespoons of the oil and 2 tablespoons of the butter in a large nonstick or cast-iron skillet and heat over medium heat until the butter has melted and the mixture begins to shimmer. Check to make sure that the bread is completely soaked through with the custard, then remove it from the custard with a fish spatula and transfer it to the pan, leaving room between each slice. Cook until the bottoms are golden brown and crispy, about 3 minutes, then flip the slices and cook until golden brown and crispy on the second side, about 3 minutes more. Transfer to a wire rack set over a baking sheet and keep warm in a 250°F oven. Repeat to soak and cook the remaining 4 slices of bread.

4. Serve the French toast topped with the maple mascarpone and compote.

Peach-Raspberry Compote

Makes about 3 cups

3 large **ripe peaches**, halved, pitted, and sliced into eighths

¼ cup **sugar**

¼ cup **peach liqueur**

1 pint **fresh raspberries**

1 teaspoon finely grated **lemon zest**

1 teaspoon fresh **lemon juice**

1. Combine the peaches and sugar in a large bowl and let sit, stirring a few times, until the juices release, at least 15 minutes and up to an hour. Transfer to a large sauté pan and cook over high heat until soft, about 5 minutes. Add the peach liqueur and cook for 1 minute longer, until the liquid has reduced and the alcohol has cooked off.

2. Remove from the heat and stir in the raspberries, lemon zest, and lemon juice. Let sit until the raspberries begin to soften, about 5 minutes. Transfer to a bowl and serve warm or at room temperature. The compote can be made up to 1 day in advance, covered, and stored in the fridge; bring to room temperature before serving.

Sophie's Chocolate Chip Pancakes

As a teenager, my daughter, like most teen girls, loved to have sleepovers. And every time we hosted those giggle-fests, I knew what my job was going to be the next morning: short-order cook. These chocolate chip pancakes were Sophie's go-to order, and I happily prepared them for her and her friends on countless weekend mornings. Now that Sophie is grown, I still make them for her every time she comes home for a visit. The girl loves chocolate, and I love making her smile. It helps to prepare the batter slightly ahead of time; letting it rest for at least 20 minutes is the secret to light and fluffy pancakes.

Makes 16 pancakes

1½ cups **all-purpose flour**

3 tablespoons **sugar**

1 teaspoon **baking powder**

½ teaspoon **baking soda**

¾ teaspoon **fine sea salt**

2 large **eggs**

1½ cups plus 3 tablespoons **buttermilk**

3 tablespoons **unsalted butter**, melted and cooled, plus more for greasing

4 ounces **semisweet chocolate**, coarsely chopped

1. Whisk together the flour, sugar, baking powder, baking soda, and salt in a large bowl until combined.

2. Whisk together the eggs and buttermilk in a small bowl until smooth. Add the wet ingredients and the melted butter to the dry ingredients and whisk until just combined. Fold in the chocolate and let the batter rest for at least 20 minutes and up to 30 minutes.

3. Heat a nonstick or cast-iron griddle or pan over medium heat. Brush the griddle or pan with butter. Drop ¼ cupfuls of the batter into the pan, making sure to leave plenty of room between each pancake for the batter to expand.

4. Cook for a minute or two, until the batter bubbles at the edges and browns on the bottom, then carefully flip the pancakes and cook for a minute or two on the second side, until the batter is completely cooked through and the pancakes are puffy and deep golden brown. Serve the pancakes as you make them, or transfer them to a baking sheet and keep warm in a 250°F oven. Repeat with the remaining batter.

Spiced Pumpkin Pancakes with Maple-Cinnamon Cream

I look forward to fall for many reasons, and as far as my cooking goes, the number one reason is pumpkin. I love pumpkin's velvety texture and sweet and earthy flavor, and I use it equally in both desserts and savory foods. These sweetly spiced pancakes are a fantastic way to celebrate the first cool, crisp mornings of fall. And if you love these pancakes and simply can't relegate them to pumpkin season? It's canned pumpkin for the win, any old month of the year. Sure, you can buy your own sugar pumpkins to roast and purée, but why do that when canned pumpkin only requires a can opener? A couple of twists of the wrist, and it's perfect every time.

Makes 12 to 16 pancakes

1½ cups **all-purpose flour**

1½ teaspoons **baking powder**

¾ teaspoon **baking soda**

¾ teaspoon **kosher salt**

1½ teaspoons **ground cinnamon**

1 teaspoon **ground ginger**

⅛ teaspoon freshly grated **nutmeg**

¾ cup **pumpkin purée**

2 large **eggs**

2 tablespoons **granulated sugar**

1 tablespoon **light brown sugar**

1½ cups **buttermilk**

1 teaspoon **pure vanilla extract**

3 tablespoons **unsalted butter**, melted, plus more for greasing

Maple-Cinnamon Cream (recipe follows), for serving

1. Whisk together the flour, baking powder, baking soda, salt, cinnamon, ginger, and nutmeg in a large bowl.

2. Whisk together the pumpkin purée, eggs, and sugars in a medium bowl until smooth. Whisk in the buttermilk and vanilla until combined. Add the wet ingredients and the melted butter to the dry ingredients and whisk until just combined. Cover the bowl and let the batter rest for 20 minutes.

3. Heat a nonstick or cast-iron griddle or pan over medium heat. Brush the griddle or pan with butter. Drop ¼ cupfuls of the batter into the pan, making sure to leave plenty of room between the pancakes for the batter to expand.

4. Cook for a minute or two, until the batter bubbles at the edges and browns on the bottom, then carefully flip and cook for a minute or two on the second side, until the batter is completely cooked through and the pancakes are puffy and deep golden brown.

5. Serve the pancakes drizzled with maple-cinnamon cream as you make them, or transfer them to a baking sheet and keep warm in a 250°F oven until ready to serve. Repeat with the remaining batter.

Maple-Cinnamon Cream

Makes about 2 cups

⅓ cup **pure maple syrup**

1 **cinnamon stick**

Pinch of **ground cinnamon**

¾ cup **buttermilk**

¾ cup **heavy cream**

3 large **egg yolks**

2 tablespoons **sugar**

1. Combine the maple syrup, cinnamon stick, and ground cinnamon in a small saucepan. Bring to a boil over high heat and cook until reduced by half (to about 3 tablespoons). Remove from the heat and let steep and cool to room temperature; discard the cinnamon stick. Set the maple syrup aside.

2. Nestle a medium bowl into a large bowl filled with ice. Combine the buttermilk and cream in a medium saucepan and bring to a simmer over low heat. Whisk together the egg yolks, sugar, and infused maple syrup in a separate medium bowl. While whisking continuously, slowly add a few ladles of the hot milk mixture to the egg yolk mixture to temper the egg. Transfer the tempered yolk mixture to the pot with the remaining milk mixture and cook, stirring continuously with a wooden spoon, until the custard thickens and coats the back of the spoon, about 6 minutes. Pour the custard into the bowl set over the ice and stir until cool.

3. Cover and refrigerate until cold and thickened before serving, about 2 hours and up to 24 hours.

Classic Spanish Tortilla with Roasted Jalapeño Pesto

Spanish tortillas (or frittatas, depending upon your country of influence) are a godsend for brunch entertaining. A classic egg dish every bit as delicious and satisfying as an omelet, a tortilla takes far less time to prepare than individual omelets ever could—you simply whisk everything up in a bowl, transfer to a nonstick or really well-seasoned cast-iron pan, and bake until puffy. You also benefit from a bit of wiggle room with timing, as tortillas, a version of which is on the menu of nearly every tapas spot in Spain, are traditionally served at room temperature. I used to serve this tortilla adorned with kicked-up parsley-based pesto at my restaurant Bolo many years ago, and now I serve it on tortillas in my home kitchens, as well as on fish tacos, grilled pork, scrambled eggs, and even homemade pizza.

Serves 6 to 8

1 cup **olive oil**

1¼ pounds **russet potatoes** (3 or 4 medium), peeled and thinly sliced on a mandoline

2 teaspoons finely chopped fresh **thyme leaves**

Kosher salt and **freshly ground black pepper**

1 medium **Spanish onion**, halved and thinly sliced

9 large **eggs**

Roasted Jalapeño Pesto (page 32), for serving

1. Heat ½ cup of the oil in a 10-inch nonstick or well-seasoned cast-iron pan over medium heat until it begins to shimmer. Add half the potatoes and one-third of the thyme and season with salt and pepper. Cook, stirring occasionally and adjusting the heat if needed, so that they do not brown, until the potatoes are tender when pierced with a paring knife, about 8 minutes. Remove the potatoes with a slotted spoon and transfer them to a colander set over a bowl. Add the remaining ½ cup oil to the pan and heat until it begins to shimmer. Add the remaining potatoes and one-third more of the thyme, season with salt and pepper, and cook as you did the first batch. Transfer the second batch of potatoes to the colander with the first and set aside.

2. Pour all but 2 tablespoons of the oil from the pan into a heatproof measuring cup and set aside. Heat the oil remaining in the pan over medium heat until it begins to shimmer. Add the onion and cook, stirring occasionally, until soft, about 5 minutes. Add the remaining thyme and season with salt and pepper.

3. Preheat the broiler.

(recipe continues)

4. Whisk together the eggs in a large bowl until lightly frothy and evenly colored, about 2 minutes. Fold the potatoes and onions into the eggs until evenly combined. In the pan you used to cook the potatoes, heat 2 tablespoons of the reserved oil over medium heat until it begins to shimmer. Add the egg mixture to the pan, making sure the potatoes and onions are evenly distributed. As soon as the edges firm up, after a minute or so, reduce the heat to medium-low. Cook until the bottom is set and light golden brown, about 5 minutes. Transfer the pan to the oven and broil until the top is puffed and lightly golden brown, 3 to 5 minutes, depending on the strength of your broiler.

5. Rub a spatula around the outside of the pan and along the bottom and slide the tortilla out onto a cutting board. Cut the tortilla into wedges and transfer to a plate. Let cool slightly.

6. Drizzle the tortilla with pesto and serve warm (not hot) or at room temperature. Do not refrigerate.

Roasted Jalapeño Pesto

Makes about 1½ cups

3 large **jalapeños**

Canola oil

Kosher salt and **freshly ground black pepper**

2 cups tightly packed fresh **flat-leaf parsley leaves**

¼ cup **pine nuts**

1 **garlic clove**, chopped

½ cup **extra-virgin olive oil**

¼ cup grated **Parmigiano Reggiano cheese**

1. Preheat the oven to 400°F.

2. In a medium bowl, toss the jalapeños with a few teaspoons of canola oil and season with salt and pepper. Spread them on a baking sheet in an even layer and roast until golden brown and charred, turning once, about 18 minutes. Return the jalapeños to the bowl, cover with plastic wrap, and let steam for 15 minutes. Peel and seed the jalapeños (discard the skin and seeds) and transfer to a food processor.

3. Add the parsley, pine nuts, and garlic to the food processor and pulse to coarsely chop. With the motor running, add the olive oil through the feed tube and process until smooth. Scrape into a bowl, fold in the cheese, and season with salt and pepper. The pesto can be stored in the refrigerator, tightly covered, for up to 2 days.

Classic Eggs Benedict Okay, so if my daughter, Sophie, isn't asking for chocolate chip pancakes (see page 27) for breakfast, then she is keeping it old-school and requesting this classic dish. Thankfully, eggs Benedict was one of the first things I learned to make at the French Culinary Institute so many years ago. Perfectly poached eggs, rich hollandaise, salty ham . . . there is a reason why this decadent dish has stood the test of time. It is definitely Sophie's favorite egg dish and, truth be told, mine, too!

Serves 4

4 **English muffins**, split

8 slices **Canadian bacon** or thick-cut ham, or 8 slices thick-cut regular bacon

8 **Poached Eggs** (page 35)

Hollandaise (page 35)

Flaky sea salt

Coarsely ground black pepper

¼ cup chopped fresh **chives**

2 tablespoons chopped fresh **dill**, tarragon, or parsley (optional)

1. Preheat the broiler.

2. Put the muffins cut-side up in a single layer on a baking sheet. Transfer to the oven and broil until golden brown, 1 to 3 minutes, depending on how powerful your broiler is. Turn the muffins over and broil until lightly browned on the second side, about 1 minute more.

3. Turn the muffins back over so that the cut side is facing up again. Top each muffin with a slice of the bacon and broil until the bacon is lightly golden brown and just warmed through, 1 to 3 minutes.

4. Top each muffin half with a poached egg and pour about ¼ cup of the hollandaise over each. Sprinkle with a bit of sea salt and pepper, garnish with the chives and dill (if using), and serve.

(recipe continues)

Poached Eggs

Makes 8 eggs

2 teaspoons **distilled white** or white wine **vinegar**

8 large **eggs**

Kosher salt and **freshly ground black pepper**

TIP Poached eggs can be made up to 1 hour in advance. After poaching, plunge the eggs into a large bowl of ice water and let stand until completely cold, about 2 minutes. Spray a baking sheet with nonstick spray, transfer the eggs to the baking sheet, and refrigerate. When ready to serve, bring 3 inches of water to a simmer in a medium pot, plunge the eggs in one at a time, and cook until just heated through and the yolk is still runny, about 20 seconds. Remove with a slotted spoon and serve.

1. Line a plate with paper towels or a clean kitchen towel. Fill a medium pot with 3 inches of water. Add the vinegar and bring to a simmer over medium heat. (Look for just a few bubbles; the water should never boil.) Gently crack an egg into a ramekin and then slowly slide it into the center of the pot, letting the water swirl around it so the white envelops the yolk. Repeat with 3 more of the eggs.

2. Cook until the whites are set but the yolks are still runny, about 4 minutes. Once the eggs are perfectly poached, remove them from the water using a slotted spoon and let drain on the paper towel–lined plate. Season the top with salt and pepper.

Hollandaise

Makes about 1¼ cups

¾ cup (1½ sticks) **unsalted butter**, cut into pieces

3 large **egg yolks**

2 teaspoons fresh **lemon juice**, plus more to taste

¼ teaspoon **cayenne pepper** or hot paprika, plus more to taste

Kosher salt and **freshly ground black pepper**

1. Melt the butter in a small pot over medium heat until foamy but not yet beginning to brown, 3 to 4 minutes. Remove from the heat.

2. Place the egg yolks and 2 teaspoons water in a blender and blend until light and frothy. With the motor running, very slowly add the hot melted butter until it has all been incorporated. (If the mixture starts to get too thick to blend, add ½ teaspoon water.) Add the lemon juice and cayenne (feel free to adjust the amounts to taste) and season with salt and black pepper. Transfer the hollandaise to a small bowl and place plastic wrap directly on the surface to prevent a skin from forming. Set aside at room temperature until ready to serve.

Variation

Introduce a bit of herby flavor to your hollandaise by adding 2 tablespoons finely chopped fresh dill, parsley, cilantro, tarragon, chives, or a combination.

Johnny Cake Waffles with Cactus Pear Syrup, Bananas, and Blackberries

My pastry chef Josephine Pacquing created this waffle with great success for a brunch event we once did at Bar Americain at Mohegan Sun. I loved her recipe so much that I now serve the waffles at home. They made a recent appearance at my annual pre–Belmont Stakes brunch, a meal I serve for friends before we head to the track for the final leg of horse racing's famed Triple Crown. If you aren't feeling the cactus pear syrup, good old pure maple syrup will work nicely, too. Just like those chocolate chip pancakes on page 27, the batter for these waffles needs to rest before cooking, but this time, it's for a good 8 hours instead of 20 minutes. Your best bet is to make the batter before bed so it's ready to go first thing in the morning.

Serves 12 to 16

1½ cups **all-purpose flour**

1½ cups fine **yellow cornmeal**

1 cup **cornstarch**

2½ tablespoons **baking powder**

2 tablespoons **sugar**

2 teaspoons **kosher salt**

3 cups **whole milk**

1 cup **sour cream**

4 large **eggs**, separated

1½ cups (3 sticks) **unsalted butter**, melted and cooled slightly

Melted butter or nonstick cooking spray, for the waffle iron

2 ripe **bananas**, peeled and sliced into ¼-inch-thick rounds

1 pint **fresh blackberries**

Cactus Pear Syrup (recipe follows), for serving

1. Whisk together the flour, cornmeal, cornstarch, baking powder, sugar, and salt in a large bowl. Whisk together the milk, sour cream, and egg yolks in a medium bowl. Add the wet ingredients and the melted butter to the dry ingredients and mix until just combined.

2. Whip the egg whites in a medium bowl with a balloon whisk until soft peaks form. Gently fold the egg whites into the batter. Cover the bowl and refrigerate for at least 8 hours and up to 12 hours.

3. Heat a waffle iron to high. Brush the waffle iron plates with butter or spray with nonstick spray. Scoop ¼ cup of the batter onto the plates and cook according to the manufacturer's directions. Transfer the waffle to a serving platter and repeat with the remaining batter.

4. Serve the waffles topped with the bananas and blackberries and drizzled with cactus pear syrup.

Cactus Pear Syrup

Makes about 1 cup

1 pound **prickly pears** (aka cactus pears)

¾ cup **sugar**

1 **cinnamon stick**

1 **star anise pod**

1 **vanilla bean**, split lengthwise and seeds scraped out

1. With the tip of a sharp knife, scrape the thorns off the prickly pears. Working with one at a time, cut off the ends of the fruit and make a lengthwise slit through the skin; peel off and discard the skin. Repeat with the remaining fruit and coarsely chop

2. Combine the prickly pear flesh and 2 cups of cold water in a medium saucepan, bring to a boil over high heat, and reduce to medium heat. Cook, stirring a few times, until the cactus pear is softened, and the mixture thickens, slightly, for about 20 minutes.

3. Transfer the mixture to a food processor and process until smooth. Strain the mixture through a fine-mesh strainer into a medium saucepan, pressing on the solids to get as much liquid out as possible. Discard the solids.

4. Add ¼ cup of water, the sugar, cinnamon stick, star anise, and vanilla bean pod and seeds to the puree. Bring the mixture to a boil over medium heat, stirring to dissolve the sugar. Reduce the heat to maintain a simmer and cook until thickened and reduced to about 1 cup, about 20 minutes. Remove from the heat and let steep for 30 minutes. Strain through a fine-mesh sieve into a bowl.

5. The sauce will keep in the refrigerator, tightly covered, for up to 3 days. Serve at room temperature or reheat in a small saucepan over low heat before serving.

NOTE These waffles freeze well. Once they're cooked, let them cool to room temperature. Wrap each cooled waffle separately in plastic wrap, then in foil. Freeze for up to 1 month. To reheat, warm in a toaster; alternatively, preheat the oven to 375°F. Place a baking sheet in the oven and heat for 5 minutes. Put the waffles in a single layer on the hot baking sheet and cook until heated through and crisp, about 5 minutes.

Classic Home Fries

I feel like people are either Team Home Fry or Team Hash Brown—the only difference being one is made with diced potatoes and the other with shredded potatoes. Not true with me—I am living proof that you can be a fan of both. Even so, I tend to make home fries more often because I'd rather dice than shred my potatoes! A few tips for perfection: Boil the potatoes first (for even texture and a creamy interior), and cook them in a combination of butter and oil for maximum flavor without burning. A cast-iron pan will help you achieve the ultimate crust.

Serves 4 to 6

Kosher salt

2½ pounds **Yukon Gold potatoes**, cut into ½-inch dice

3 tablespoons **canola oil**

1 medium **Spanish onion**, halved and thinly sliced

3 tablespoons **unsalted butter**

Freshly ground black pepper

¼ cup thinly sliced fresh **chives**

1. Bring a large pot of water to a boil over high heat. Add 2 tablespoons salt and the potatoes and cook until just tender, about 8 minutes. Drain well in a colander.

2. Heat 1 tablespoon of the oil in a large cast-iron skillet over medium heat until it begins to shimmer. Add the onion and cook, stirring a few times, until soft and lightly golden brown, about 5 minutes. Transfer the onion to a plate.

3. Add the remaining 2 tablespoons oil and the butter to the pan. Increase the heat to high and heat until the butter has melted and the oil is sizzling. Add the potatoes, season with salt and pepper, and immediately use a wide metal spatula to press them into an even layer on the bottom of the pan. Cook, pressing down occasionally but not turning them, until the potatoes on the bottom are golden brown and crusty, about 5 minutes. Turn the potatoes over, press down again, and cook until the potatoes on the bottom are golden brown, about 5 minutes more. Stir in the onion and season with salt and pepper.

4. Transfer to a shallow bowl or a platter, garnish with the chives, and serve.

Variations

Red Chile Home Fries Follow the recipe as written, but in step 3, after adding the potatoes to the pan, stir in 1 tablespoon ancho chile powder and ¼ teaspoon cayenne pepper along with the salt and black pepper, and stir in ¼ cup chopped fresh cilantro leaves with the onion at the end.

Fresh Herbs Follow the recipe as written, but in step 3, stir in ¼ cup chopped fresh herbs along with the onion.

Perfect Scrambled Eggs

Perfect Scrambled Eggs Easiest thing in the world, right? Sure, anyone can scramble eggs, but *perfect* scrambled eggs? There are a few tricks of the trade to this: First, use a nonstick pan. Second, cook over low heat. Give yourself a little time. Third, undercook them! Cut the flame just before you think your eggs are done, and let the carryover heat finish cooking them. Fourth, butter. Lots of butter. That, plus a touch of crème fraîche. Fifth, do not season with salt until the very end (the salt can make the egg toughen). Follow these rules, and you will never have flabby, rubbery scrambled eggs again.

Serves 4

12 large **eggs**

4 tablespoons (½ stick) cold **unsalted butter**, cut into small pieces

¼ cup **crème fraîche**

Kosher salt and **freshly ground black pepper**

Flavorings of your choice (optional)

1. Crack the eggs into a large bowl and whisk until light, frothy, and uniform in color. Strain the eggs through a fine-mesh strainer into a separate bowl.

2. Combine the butter and crème fraîche in a large nonstick sauté pan. Pour the eggs into the pan and turn the heat to low and cook slowly; mix gently using a heat-resistant rubber spatula or a wooden spoon until soft curds form, about 6 minutes. Remove from the heat (the eggs will still be somewhat wet). Season with salt and pepper, and add any flavoring additions you'd like (pictured opposite with goat cheese, chives, and romesco). Let stand for 1 minute more to allow the heat of the pan to finish cooking the eggs. Serve immediately.

Additional Flavorings

Gently fold in any of these additions just as the eggs are coming off the heat:

- ¼ cup thinly sliced scallions
- 2 tablespoons finely chopped fresh chives
- ½ cup crumbled goat cheese
- ¼ cup romesco sauce (see page 54)
- 4 ounces bûcheron cheese

Roasted Strawberries with Clotted Cream and Toasted Almonds

Strawberries with whipped cream is very "breakfast at Wimbledon," and in the summer months when strawberries are at their peak, that is how I serve them—nice and simple. Even though you can get strawberries twelve months out of the year, they're not always at their top form. So if I get a strawberry craving in January, when those berries could use some help, I turn to this recipe. Roasting the berries 'til they're soft and caramelized transforms otherwise lackluster fruit into sugary-sweet gems. They're delicious any day of the year, especially when served with a dollop of clotted cream (or Greek yogurt) and a sprinkling of toasted almonds for some crunch.

Serves 4 to 6

1 quart **strawberries**, hulled

½ cup **sugar**

1 tablespoon fresh **lemon juice**

½ cup **clotted cream** or Greek yogurt

½ cup chopped **almonds**, lightly toasted

1. Preheat the oven to 400°F.

2. Combine the strawberries, sugar, and lemon juice in a large bowl. Let sit, stirring a few times, until the strawberries release their juices, about 20 minutes.

3. Transfer the strawberries and their juices to a rimmed baking sheet and bake until the strawberries are soft and the juices are bubbling, about 15 minutes.

4. Spoon the strawberries into bowls, top with a dollop of clotted cream and a scattering of almonds, and serve.

NOTE You can buy clotted cream in specialty stores in the same area you'd find sour cream and cream cheese. Whipped cream cheese also makes a great substitute.

Pomegranate-Glazed Bacon

I started glazing bacon when I wrote my book *Brunch @ Bobby's* several years ago. Up until that time, I just baked it on its own—I never thought I needed to mess with a good thing. Boy, let me tell you—was I ever wrong about that. Glazing bacon with something sweet like maple syrup, sorghum syrup, or pomegranate molasses (one of my favorite ingredients) creates the ultimate salty-sweet indulgence. I almost never serve bacon without a glaze anymore. I am guessing after you try this, you won't, either.

Serves 4 to 6

1 pound **thick-cut bacon**
(about 12 slices)

¾ cup **pomegranate molasses**

2 tablespoons **Dijon mustard**

¼ teaspoon **coarsely ground black pepper**

1. Preheat the oven to 400°F.

2. Lay the bacon in a single layer on a rimmed baking sheet, leaving ¼ inch between each slice. Bake until lightly browned and crisp, 15 to 20 minutes.

3. While the bacon is cooking, whisk together the pomegranate molasses, mustard, and pepper in a medium bowl until smooth. Set the glaze aside.

4. Remove the bacon from the oven. Carefully drain the fat into a medium bowl. Place the baking sheet on a wire rack and immediately brush each slice of bacon with the glaze. Let sit at room temperature until the glaze has set and cooled slightly, about 10 minutes, then serve immediately.

Variations

Brown Sugar–Pecan Line the baking sheet with a silicone baking mat or parchment paper. Divide ¾ cup packed light brown sugar evenly over the top of the bacon slices and bake until the bacon is golden brown and almost crispy, about 13 minutes. Remove from the oven and sprinkle with ⅓ cup finely chopped pecans. Return to the oven and bake until the pecans are toasted and the bacon is crispy, about 3 minutes more. Let sit at room temperature for 10 minutes before serving.

Red Chile–Honey Whisk together ¾ cup clover honey and 2 tablespoons ancho chile powder in a small bowl. Follow the recipe as written, but use the honey-chile mixture instead of the pomegranate glaze.

Sorghum Follow the recipe as written, but use ¾ cup sorghum syrup instead of the pomegranate glaze.

SNACKS + APPETIZERS

As a host, I think it's imperative to provide something to hold your guests over until the main event. Whether you go big with a gorgeous Mediterranean Mezze Platter of luscious dips and spreads (see page 55) or practice restraint with a simple bowl of can't-stop-won't-stop Maple-Chile Glazed Nuts (page 74), a premeal bite keeps everyone happy. So often it's the smallest bites with the biggest impact and the appetizers are the best part of the meal. I could plant myself in front of the Avocado Relish with Roasted Green Chile Pesto (page 64) or a hot *cazuela* of Baked Manchego with Yellow Pepper Romesco (page 53) and call it a night. If deviled eggs are your thing, you're in luck. I have a master recipe (see page 48) that transports me to the legendary cocktail parties of my parents' generation, plus a twist (see page 49) that might make it into your own family's culinary memory bank.

Deviled Egg Master Recipe

Deviled eggs were one of the first things I learned to make as a child; my job was to mix the yolks with the mayonnaise and mustard. I serve these eggs often at get-togethers at my home, and they are always the first thing to go. I would serve them more, but I hate peeling eggs!

Makes 24 deviled eggs

½ cup **mayonnaise**, such as Hellmann's

1 heaping tablespoon **Dijon mustard**

1 teaspoon **white wine vinegar**

½ teaspoon **kosher salt**

¼ teaspoon **freshly ground black pepper**

12 **Perfect Hard-Cooked Eggs** (recipe follows), chilled and peeled

Smoked paprika, for garnish

1. Whisk together the mayonnaise, mustard, vinegar, salt, and pepper in a small bowl until smooth.

2. Slice each egg in half lengthwise. Carefully remove the yolks and place them in a large bowl. Set the whites on a plate or platter, cut-side up, and set aside.

3. Using a fork, mash the yolks into fine crumbles. Add the mayonnaise mixture and mix well.

4. Evenly divide heaping teaspoons of the yolk mixture among the egg whites or scrape the mixture into a pastry bag with a starred or plain tip and pipe the mixture among the whites. Sprinkle with paprika and serve. If not serving the eggs immediately, cover and store in the refrigerator for up to 1 day.

Variations

Green Eggs Fold ¼ cup finely diced dill pickle and ¼ cup finely chopped fresh dill into the yolk filling.

Red Chile Eggs Add 1 tablespoon ancho chile powder to the mayonnaise mixture and whisk until smooth.

Perfect Hard-Cooked Eggs

Makes 12 eggs

No matter how you decide to spin the filling, the best deviled eggs all start with a perfectly cooked egg. I can't take credit for this method— it was created by the one and only Julia Child and, no surprise, it is foolproof every time.

12 large **eggs**

1. Carefully place the eggs in a single layer in the bottom of a large saucepan. Cover with cold water by 2 inches. Bring the water to a boil over high heat and cook for 1 minute. Remove the pan from the heat and cover. Let sit for exactly 17 minutes (set a timer). Meanwhile, fill a large bowl with ice and water.

2. When the timer goes off, drain the eggs and immediately transfer them to the prepared ice bath. Let them sit until chilled through, at least 15 minutes. Peel under cold running water and pat dry. If not using the eggs immediately, place them in a bowl, cover, and store in the refrigerator for up to 2 days.

Deviled Eggs with Cornichon Rémoulade

Adding a few different ingredients to the mayonnaise base is easy, and takes the master recipe to another level of deliciousness. When I want to be extra fancy, I love topping each deviled egg with a Pickled Shrimp or a Fried Oyster plus a drizzle of hot sauce.

Makes 24 deviled eggs

12 **Perfect Hard-Cooked Eggs**
   (page 48), chilled and peeled

1 cup prepared **mayonnaise**

2 tablespoons **whole-grain mustard**

4 **cornichons**, finely diced

3 tablespoons finely chopped
   fresh **dill**

2 tablespoons finely sliced fresh
   chives

½ teaspoon **kosher salt**

¼ teaspoon **freshly ground black
   pepper**

24 **Pickled Shrimp** or **Fried Oysters**
   (page 50)

Fresh **flat-leaf parsley leaves**, for
   garnish

Smoked paprika, for garnish

1. Slice each egg in half lengthwise. Carefully remove the yolks and place them in a large bowl. Set the whites on a plate or platter, cut-side up, and set aside.

2. Using a fork, mash the yolks into fine crumbles. Add the mayonnaise and mix well. Fold in the mustard, cornichons, dill, chives, salt, and pepper.

3. Evenly divide heaping teaspoons of the yolk mixture among the egg whites. Top each egg with a shrimp or a fried oyster. Garnish each egg with a parsley leaf and a pinch of smoked paprika, and serve.

(recipe continues)

Pickled Shrimp

Makes about 30 shrimp

These shrimp are great sitting atop a Deviled Egg (page 49), added to a salad, or simply served in a bowl with toothpicks at a cocktail party. I add a little bit of hot sauce and a few chiles de árbol for some spice, but the recipe is still great minus the spice.

1 (2-inch) piece **lemon zest**

1 cup fresh **lemon juice**

1 cup **cider vinegar**

2 **garlic cloves**, thinly sliced

½ **Vidalia onion**, thinly sliced

2 tablespoons **pickling spice**

2 tablespoons **sugar**

2 **whole dried chiles de árbol**, or ¼ teaspoon crushed red pepper flakes or a few dashes of hot sauce

Kosher salt

6 sprigs **flat-leaf parsley**

2 pounds medium **shrimp** (26 to 30 count), peeled and deveined

1. Combine the lemon zest and juice, vinegar, garlic, onion, pickling spice, sugar, chiles, 1 tablespoon salt, and ½ cup water in a medium saucepan. Bring to a boil over high heat and cook for 1 minute. Reduce the heat to maintain a simmer and cook for 4 minutes more. Transfer the pickling liquid to a large heatproof bowl and let cool to room temperature.

2. Bring a large pot of water, 2 tablespoons salt, and the parsley to a boil. Fill a large bowl with ice and water and set it nearby. Add the shrimp and immediately remove the pot from the heat. Cover and let sit for 5 minutes. Drain the shrimp and plunge them into the ice water to stop the cooking; let cool. Drain the shrimp and pat dry.

3. Add the cooked shrimp to the bowl with the pickling liquid, cover, and refrigerate for at least 4 hours and up to 24 hours before serving, stirring several times. To serve, remove the shrimp with a slotted spoon from the pickling liquid.

Fried Oysters

Makes 24 oysters

24 **oysters**, shucked and patted dry

Kosher salt and **freshly ground black pepper**

2 cups fine **yellow cornmeal**

Canola oil

1. Set a wire rack over a baking sheet and place it nearby. Season the oysters with salt and pepper. Place the cornmeal in a medium bowl and season with salt and pepper. Dredge each oyster in the cornmeal, tapping off any excess.

2. Fill a medium high-sided sauté pan with 1 inch of oil. Heat the oil over medium heat until shimmering. Working in batches, fry the oysters until golden brown on both sides, about 1 minute each side. Transfer to the rack on the baking sheet and immediately season with a pinch of salt. Repeat with the remaining oysters.

Baked Manchego with Yellow Pepper Romesco

This dish was a mainstay at my Spanish-inspired restaurant Bolo, where *cazuelas* (sturdy clay cookware that hails from Spain) of the nutty, almond-crusted cheese poured out of the kitchen, delighting hungry diners 'til the restaurant's closing in 2007. It's like the best, most sophisticated mozzarella stick you never even knew you could have. Garlicky, vinegary yellow pepper romesco begs to be slathered over each warm bite of cheese, its intensity instantly mellowed by the buttery Manchego. A sliced baguette may be an optional addition, but one I recommend—people are going to want an edible vehicle for getting each and every bit from the dish to their mouths, and stat.

Serves 4 to 6

¼ cup **all-purpose flour**

Kosher salt and **freshly ground black pepper**

2 large **eggs**

¾ cup **panko bread crumbs**

¼ cup finely **ground almonds**

2 (8-ounce) slices **Manchego cheese**, each about 1 inch thick

2 tablespoons **olive oil**

2 tablespoons **almond oil** (or more olive oil)

Yellow Pepper Romesco (page 54)

Baguette, thinly sliced (optional)

1. Put the flour in a shallow bowl and season with salt and pepper. Put the eggs in a separate shallow bowl, add 2 tablespoons water, and season with salt and pepper. Whisk until smooth. Combine the panko and almonds on a large plate.

2. Dredge the cheese slices in the flour and tap off any excess. Dip them into the egg wash, letting the excess drip off, then dredge them in the panko mixture, pressing the crumbs into the cheese to adhere. Set aside on a plate.

3. Line a plate with paper towels and set it nearby. Heat the oils in a large nonstick pan over high heat until they begin to shimmer. Add the breaded cheese to the hot oil and fry until golden brown on both sides and softened, about 3 minutes per side. Transfer the cheese to the paper towel–lined plate and season with a sprinkling of salt.

4. Put some of the romesco into the bottom of two *cazuelas*, a serving platter, or a baking dish. Top with the cheese. Serve with baguette slices on the side, if desired.

(recipe continues)

Yellow Pepper Romesco

Makes about 2 cups

Olive oil

6 **garlic cloves**

¼ cup **whole almonds**

1 slice **white bread**, crust removed, cut into small cubes

1 **yellow bell pepper**, roasted, peeled, and seeded (see Tip)

2 **yellow tomatoes**, halved and seeded

1 **ancho chile**, soaked in boiling water until soft, drained, seeded, and coarsely chopped

1 **New Mexico chile**, soaked in boiling water until soft, drained, seeded, and coarsely chopped

¼ cup **white wine vinegar**

1 tablespoon **clover honey**

Kosher salt and **freshly ground black pepper**

TIP

How to Roast Peppers and Chiles
Preheat the oven to 400°F. Place the peppers or chiles on a rimmed baking sheet. Brush with canola oil and season with salt and pepper. Roast, rotating once or twice, until charred on all sides, about 15 to 25 minutes. Transfer the peppers to a bowl and tightly cover with plastic wrap. Let steam for 15 minutes to loosen the skin, then peel, halve, and seed the peppers. Roasted peppers and chiles can be stored, tightly covered, for up to 5 days in the refrigerator.

1. Heat a few tablespoons of oil in a large sauté pan over high heat. Add the garlic and cook, stirring a few times, until lightly golden brown on both sides, about 3 minutes. Transfer to a food processor.

2. Add a few teaspoons more oil to the pan. Add the almonds and cook, stirring a few times, until lightly golden brown on both sides, about 3 minutes. Transfer to the food processor. Add the bread to the pan and cook, stirring a few times, until golden brown on both sides, about 3 minutes. Add the bread to the food processor. Add a few teaspoons more oil to the pan. Add the bell pepper and tomatoes and cook, stirring a few times, until the tomatoes are soft, about 5 minutes. Transfer to the food processor.

3. Add the chiles, vinegar, and honey to the food processor and process until smooth. Add more olive oil, if needed, to achieve a paste consistency. Taste and season with salt and black pepper.

4. Scrape the romesco sauce into a bowl. The romesco will keep in the refrigerator, tightly covered, for up to 1 day.

Mediterranean Mezze Platter I adore the cuisine of the Mediterranean, and as much as it is the food itself, it's the style of eating that I find so appealing. A mezze platter is such a great way to get to taste a little of this, a little of that, and really makes dining a communal experience. It's also an easy place to turn out all the odds and ends of your produce or cheese drawer! No mezze platter would be complete without a good dip or two, and this Meyer lemon hummus and tzatziki spiked with green olive pesto are my particular favorites. So satisfying and full of flavor, you don't even register how healthy and packed with fiber and protein they are. Plus, this is such an easy dish to whip up for guests—if you decide to forgo the homemade za'atar pita chips for store-bought ones, you don't even need to turn on your oven.

Serves 4 to 6

8 whole **pocketless pitas**, cut into eighths

Canola oil

¼ cup **za'atar**

Kosher salt

Meyer Lemon Hummus (page 56)

Tzatziki with Green Olive Pesto (page 56)

Fresh vegetables (such as carrots, bell peppers, green beans, and celery), for dipping (optional)

1. Preheat the oven to 350°F.

2. Put the pita pieces in an even layer on a large baking sheet (you may need two baking sheets). Brush with the oil on one side and season with the za'atar and salt. Bake until lightly golden brown and crisp, about 10 minutes.

3. Serve the pita chips with the hummus, tzatziki, and vegetables, if desired, on the side.

(recipe continues)

Meyer Lemon Hummus

Makes about 3 cups

1 teaspoon **ground cumin**

1 teaspoon **hot smoked paprika**

¼ teaspoon **cayenne pepper**

2 (15.5-ounce) cans **chickpeas**, drained and rinsed

2 **garlic cloves**, finely chopped to a paste with the side of a chef's knife and ¼ teaspoon kosher salt

1 **serrano chile**, chopped

¼ cup **top-quality tahini**

¼ cup **Meyer lemon juice**

½ cup **extra-virgin olive oil**, plus more for serving

1 tablespoon **toasted sesame oil**

1 teaspoon finely grated **Meyer lemon zest**

Kosher salt and **freshly ground black pepper**

¼ cup finely chopped fresh **flat-leaf parsley leaves**

1. Combine the cumin, paprika, and cayenne in a small sauté pan and cook over medium-low heat, stirring continuously, until fragrant, about 3 minutes. Remove from the heat and set aside.

2. Combine half the chickpeas, the garlic, serrano, tahini, lemon juice, olive oil, and sesame oil in a food processor and process until smooth. Season with the lemon zest, salt, and pepper and scrape into a large bowl.

3. Put the remaining chickpeas in a medium bowl and coarsely mash using a fork or potato masher. Fold the coarsely mashed chickpeas and parsley into the mixture in the large bowl.

4. Transfer the hummus to a serving bowl. Drizzle with a few tablespoons of olive oil and serve.

Tzatziki with Green Olive Pesto

Makes about 3 cups

1 cup **pitted green olives**, such as Picholine

½ cup chopped fresh **flat-leaf parsley leaves**

2 tablespoons **pine nuts**

2 tablespoons grated **Parmigiano Reggiano cheese**

¼ cup **extra-virgin olive oil**, plus more for garnish

2 cups **2% Greek yogurt**, such as Fage

2 **Kirby cucumbers**, coarsely grated and drained on paper towels

3 **garlic cloves**, chopped to a paste with the side of a chef's knife and ¼ teaspoon kosher salt

2 tablespoons finely chopped fresh **dill**, plus more for garnish

Kosher salt and **freshly ground black pepper**

1. Combine the pitted olives, parsley, pine nuts, cheese, and oil in a food processor and process until smooth. Scrape into a bowl. (The pesto can be made up to 2 days in advance, covered, and stored in the refrigerator until ready to serve.)

2. Combine the yogurt, cucumbers, garlic, and dill in a medium bowl and season with salt and pepper.

3. Transfer the yogurt mixture to a medium serving bowl and swirl in the pesto. Drizzle the top with a few tablespoons extra-virgin olive oil and garnish with additional dill. If not serving immediately, tightly cover the dip and store in the refrigerator for up to 1 day.

Tomato Bread with Serrano Ham and Parsley Pesto

You see *pan con tomate*—"bread with tomato"—in every tapas bar in Spain, with good reason: it is delicious. It also happens to be one of the easiest appetizers you will ever make. Like so many simple recipes, though, keep in mind that when there are so few ingredients, each one must be perfect. That's especially true of the tomato in this dish: it needs to be overly ripe and practically bursting with flavor. For almost all of us, that means this is a very season-specific dish, best served in late summer when tomatoes are at their peak.

Serves 4 to 6

PARSLEY PESTO

⅓ cup **extra-virgin olive oil**

2 **garlic cloves**, finely chopped to a paste using the side of a chef's knife and ¼ teaspoon kosher salt

Kosher salt and **freshly ground black pepper**

¼ cup lightly packed finely chopped fresh **flat-leaf parsley leaves**

1 tablespoon finely chopped **pine nuts**

3 overly ripe large **beefsteak tomatoes**

Kosher salt and **freshly ground black pepper**

Pinch of **crushed red pepper flakes** (optional)

1 loaf **ciabatta**, cut into ¼-inch-thick slices

2 large **garlic cloves**, sliced in half

¼ cup **extra-virgin olive oil**

¼ pound thinly sliced **serrano ham**

1. **Make the parsley pesto:** Stir together the oil and garlic in a small bowl and season with salt and pepper. Add the parsley and pine nuts and mix until just combined. Set aside.

2. Cut the tomatoes in half horizontally. Place a box grater in a large bowl. Rub the cut side of the tomato halves over the large holes of the box grater, using the flattened palm of your hand to move the tomatoes back and forth. The flesh should be grated off, leaving the skin intact in your hand. Discard the skin and season the tomato pulp with salt, black pepper, and red pepper flakes (if using). Let sit at room temperature while you prepare the bread.

3. Heat a grill to high or heat a grill pan over high heat. Grill the bread, cut-side down, until lightly charred and golden brown, about 1 minute. Flip the bread and grill for 30 seconds more to just heat through. Rub the cut sides of the garlic cloves over the cut side of the bread and brush with the olive oil.

4. Spoon liberal amounts of the tomato pulp onto the bread and drizzle with the pesto. Top with the ham slices. Serve at room temperature.

Rough-Cut Tuna Nachos with Avocado Crema

This is a playful and lighter spin on classic nachos and a simpler version of the very popular dish that is on the menu at Mesa Grill Las Vegas. I make the sauce and chips from scratch at the restaurant, but at home, it's bottled mango-habanero sauce and high-quality tortilla chips from a bag—even chefs enjoy shortcuts from time to time. Serve with ice-cold pitchers of margaritas (see page 226).

Serves 4 to 6

AVOCADO CREMA

2 ripe **Hass avocados**, pitted, peeled, and chopped

2 **garlic cloves**, chopped

2 **jalapeños**, roasted, peeled, and chopped (see Tip; page 54)

Juice of 2 limes

Kosher salt and **freshly ground black pepper**

2 tablespoons **Dijon mustard**

2 tablespoons **olive oil**

2 teaspoons **puréed chipotle chile in adobo** (see Note)

1½ pounds **fresh tuna**, cut into ½-inch dice

3 tablespoons **capers**, drained

¼ cup chopped fresh **cilantro**, plus more for garnish

¼ cup finely sliced **scallions**

Kosher salt and **freshly ground black pepper**

¼ cup **mango-habanero hot sauce**, for serving

Blue and white corn **tortilla chips**, for serving

1. **Make the avocado crema:** Place the avocado, garlic, jalapeños, lime juice, and ¼ cup cold water in a blender. Season with salt and pepper and blend until smooth, adding a bit more water if needed to achieve the desired consistency. Set aside.

2. Whisk together the mustard, oil, and chipotle purée in a large bowl until combined. Add the tuna, capers, cilantro, and scallions and gently fold to combine.

3. Mound the tuna in the center of the platter. Serve with the avocado crema, mango hot sauce, and chips on the side. (Alternatively, spread the crema and hot sauce on the platter under the tuna.)

NOTE To make chipotle in adobo purée, empty a can of chipotles in adobo into a blender, rinse the can with cold water and add half of the water to the blender and blend until smooth. Scrape into a bowl. The purée will last in an airtight container up to 1 month in the refrigerator and up to 3 months in the freezer.

Brussels Sprout Nachos with Pickled Chiles

I made these hearty vegetarian nachos for a Super Bowl party a few years ago and was shocked at how much people loved the dish. Not shocked because I didn't think it was good—never doubted that—but because I was sure my friends were going to miss the meat of the classic version and rib me for the "newfangled" offering. One bite was enough to knock any potential naysayers to the ground. Brussels sprouts are the darling of the vegetable world and have been for some time, but if you still think you don't like them, try this recipe—it's a touchdown.

Serves 4

MUENSTER CHEESE SAUCE

2 tablespoons **unsalted butter**

2 tablespoons **all-purpose flour**

2 cups **whole milk**, warmed

8 ounces **Muenster cheese**, finely chopped

Kosher salt and **freshly ground black pepper**

Hot sauce

1 (8.25-ounce) bag blue corn **tortilla chips**

3 tablespoons **olive oil** or vegetable oil

12 ounces **Brussels sprouts** (24 medium), trimmed and thinly sliced

Kosher salt and **freshly ground black pepper**

Pickled Red Onions (page 248)

Pickled Chiles (page 249)

¼ cup chopped fresh **cilantro leaves**, for garnish

Finely grated **lime zest**, for garnish

1. **Make the cheese sauce:** In a medium saucepan, melt the butter over medium-high heat. Add the flour and cook, whisking continuously, until the mixture is pale blond, about 2 minutes. Slowly whisk in the milk and cook, whisking continuously, until the sauce has thickened and the raw flour taste has been cooked out, 5 to 6 minutes. Reduce the heat to low and add the cheese. Let sit without stirring for 1 minute, then whisk until smooth. Season with salt, pepper, and hot sauce. Cover and keep warm.

2. Preheat the oven to 200°F.

3. Spread the tortilla chips in an even layer over a large baking sheet. Heat the chips in the oven, about 8 to 10 minutes, while you prepare the rest of the dish.

4. Heat the oil in a large nonstick skillet over medium-high heat. Add the Brussels sprouts and cook, stirring occasionally, until tender and crisp, about 5 minutes. Season with salt and pepper.

5. Pour some of the warm cheese sauce onto a large platter. Top with a layer of the warm chips and more sauce. Sprinkle some of the Brussels sprouts and pickled onions and chiles over the sauce, then repeat all the layers once more. Garnish with the cilantro and lime zest and serve.

Avocado Relish with Roasted Green Chile Pesto

Whether you call it guacamole or avocado relish, this dip is always a hit at a party. It's safe to say that a version has been in each of my books—and this book is no exception. I want to keep my guests happy, and avocado relish is a time-tested way to do it. Looking to add a little drama to your gathering? Try mixing it up tableside in a stone *molcajete* like servers do in Mexican restaurants. I have another way to keep things new and exciting: instead of the usual chopped green chiles and cilantro leaves, I combine both into a pesto that's swirled throughout the creamy avocados. This just might be my best version yet.

Serves 4 to 6

7 large ripe **Hass avocados**, halved and pitted

1 small **red onion**, finely diced

Juice of 2 limes

Roasted Green Chile Pesto (recipe follows)

Cilantro leaves, for garnish

Pickled Red Onions (page 248), for garnish (optional)

Blue, yellow, or white corn **tortilla chips**, heated in the oven for 5 minutes

Scoop the avocado flesh into a large bowl and add the onion and lime juice. Using a fork, coarsely mash the ingredients together. Fold in the pesto. Transfer to a serving bowl and garnish with cilantro leaves and pickled red onions (if using). Serve with the tortilla chips on the side.

Roasted Green Chile Pesto

Makes about 1½ cups

1 small **poblano chile**

2 **jalapeños**

1 tablespoon plus ½ cup **canola oil**

Kosher salt and **freshly ground black pepper**

2 cups packed fresh **cilantro leaves**

¼ cup hulled **pumpkin seeds** or pine nuts

1 teaspoon finely grated **lime zest**

1. Preheat the oven to 400°F.

2. In a small bowl, toss the poblano and jalapeños with 1 tablespoon of the oil and season with salt and pepper. Transfer to a baking sheet and roast until blistered and soft, turning once, about 25 minutes. Transfer the chiles to a bowl, cover with plastic wrap, and let steam for 15 minutes. Peel and seed the chiles and transfer the flesh to a food processor; discard the skin and seeds.

3. Add the cilantro and pumpkin seeds to the food processor and pulse to coarsely chop. With the motor running, add the remaining ½ cup oil through the feed tube and process until smooth. Add the lime zest, taste, and season with salt and pepper. Pulse a few more times to combine.

4. Scrape the pesto into a bowl. The pesto will keep in the refrigerator, tightly covered in an airtight container, for up to 3 days or in the freezer for up to 1 month.

Almost-Homemade Garlic Potato Chips

I love homemade potato chips as much as the next person—but while I make them in my restaurants often, I rarely do at home. There are enough high-quality brands of potato chips on the market today that have done the dirty work for you (and with all the oil you need to make them, the splatter, the disposal, I do mean dirty). It's easy enough to "refresh" bagged chips in the oven, and serving them warm is a great way to fool your guests into thinking they were made from scratch. And that's not *completely* false—the spice blends are a great way to use up the last bits in your spice jars, and freshly toasted garlic bring an unmistakably homemade touch to this addictive, savory snack.

Serves 4 to 6

½ cup **canola oil**

8 **garlic cloves**, sliced paper thin on a mandoline or with a very sharp knife

Kosher salt

1 teaspoon **dry mustard**

1 teaspoon **ancho chile powder**

1 bag of your favorite plain, unsalted, **kettle-cooked potato chips**

1. Preheat the oven to 350°F.

2. Line a plate with paper towels and set it nearby. Heat the oil in a small sauté pan over medium heat until it begins to shimmer. Add the garlic and cook, stirring several times to keep the slices from sticking, until light golden brown, about 2 minutes. Use a slotted spoon to transfer the garlic chips to the paper towel–lined plate and season with salt. Let cool completely, about 10 minutes. (Let the garlic-infused oil cool and save it to brush on grilled bread or toast or on chicken or steak before grilling. It will keep in the refrigerator, tightly covered, for up to 1 month.)

3. Transfer the garlic chips to a spice grinder and grind to a fine powder. Transfer to a small bowl and stir in the mustard, ancho chile powder, and 1 teaspoon salt.

4. Spread the potato chips in an even layer on a large baking sheet. Bake until heated through, turning once, about 5 minutes. Remove from the oven, sprinkle with the garlic mixture, and gently toss to combine. Serve warm.

Pimento Cheese with Herb Crackers

I've often heard pimento cheese called "the caviar of the South," and while I'm not sure that's how I would choose to describe it, I will say this: this blended dip of cheddar cheese and roasted red peppers is flat-out delicious. Not only that, the Southern spread is actually quite versatile—it's great with chips or crackers, slathered on a burger, or spread between slices of bread for a perfect grilled cheese. I also like mixing it up (literally) with a more Southwestern-inspired version starring Monterey Jack cheese and roasted poblano chiles.

Serves 4 to 6

1 cup **mayonnaise**, such as Hellmann's

½ teaspoon **kosher salt**

½ teaspoon **freshly ground black pepper**

½ teaspoon **cayenne pepper**

12 ounces **extra-sharp white cheddar cheese**, coarsely grated

12 ounces **extra-sharp yellow cheddar cheese**, coarsely grated

1 cup finely diced **roasted red peppers**

Herb Crackers (recipe follows)

Whisk together the mayonnaise, salt, black pepper, and cayenne in a large bowl. Add both cheeses and the roasted red peppers and fold to combine. Cover and refrigerate for at least 30 minutes and up to 24 hours to allow the flavors to meld. Let stand at room temperature for 30 minutes before serving with the crackers.

Variation

Monterey Jack and Roasted Poblano Cheese Follow the recipe as written, but use 12 ounces Monterey Jack cheese (coarsely grated) instead of the yellow cheddar cheese and 2 large roasted poblano chiles (peeled, seeded, and finely diced) instead of the roasted red peppers.

Herb Crackers

Makes about 40 crackers

¼ cup (½ stick) **unsalted butter**

2 tablespoons finely chopped **herbs** (parsley, cilantro, or chives, or a combination)

1 teaspoon **kosher salt**

⅛ teaspoon **freshly ground black pepper**

One sleeve of **saltine crackers** (about 40, depending on the brand)

1. Preheat the oven to 325°F.

2. Melt the butter in a small saucepan over medium heat. Remove from heat and stir in the herbs, salt, and pepper. Evenly spread the crackers out on a baking sheet and brush with the herb butter. Bake until lightly golden, 5 to 7 minutes. Let cool before serving.

Crostini for Every Season

Crostini, which means "little crusts" in Italian, is probably the easiest appetizer you can make and is endlessly adaptable. If you can put it on a fork, you can put it on crostini! Start with good bread, then let your imagination run wild.

Perfect Crostini

Makes about 40 crostini

1 **French baguette** or ciabatta, sliced ¼ inch thick

¾ cup **olive oil**

Kosher salt and **freshly ground black pepper**

NOTE In the summer, I prefer to grill the bread slices: Heat a grill to high. Brush both sides of each slice of bread with the oil and season with salt and pepper. Grill until lightly golden brown and slightly charred on each side, about 30 seconds per side.

1. Preheat the oven to 350°F.

2. Arrange the baguette slices on two large rimmed baking sheets; brush both sides with the oil and season with salt and pepper. Bake until lightly golden brown, about 15 minutes, rotating the baking sheets halfway through (if the undersides are not browning, turn the crostini over once during baking). (Alternatively, preheat the broiler and broil the crostini until lightly golden brown on each side, about 1 minute per side.) Let cool on the baking sheets.

3. Top the crostini as desired (recipes follow) and serve.

Creamy Feta, Marinated Tomato, and Dill Crostini

Makes 40 crostini

I serve this to guests all summer long in the Hamptons. Within walking distance of my home, I have a farmer's market that sells the juiciest tomatoes and the most fragrant herbs.

¼ cup **red wine vinegar**

1 **garlic clove**, smashed

12 ounces assorted **heirloom cherry tomatoes**, quartered

¼ cup **extra-virgin olive oil** (preferably Greek)

¼ cup chopped fresh **dill**, plus more for garnish (optional)

5 ounces **Greek feta cheese**

¼ cup **heavy cream**

Grated **zest of 1 lemon**

Kosher salt and **freshly ground black pepper**

Perfect Crostini (left)

1. Combine the vinegar and garlic in a medium bowl and let sit for 10 minutes. Remove the garlic, add the tomatoes, oil, and dill, and let sit at room temperature for at least 30 minutes and up to 1 hour before serving.

2. Combine the feta, cream, and lemon zest in a food processor and process until smooth. Season with salt and pepper and scrape into a medium bowl.

3. Spread a few teaspoons of the feta mixture onto each slice of bread. Use a slotted spoon to add some marinated tomatoes to each crostini, top each with extra dill, if desired, and serve.

(recipe continues)

Fava Bean, Romano, and Lemon Crostini

Makes 40 crostini

Fava beans are a pain in the neck to prepare, but fresh ones are only available for a short time each year, and they are delicious.

Kosher salt

2 cups shelled fresh **fava beans**

2 tablespoons **extra-virgin olive oil**

Finely grated **zest and juice of 1 lemon**

Coarsely ground black pepper

¼ cup chopped fresh **mint** or parsley, for garnish

Shaved **Pecorino Romano cheese**

Perfect Crostini (page 71)

1. Fill a large bowl with ice and a few cups of cold water and set it nearby. Bring a medium pot of water to a boil. Add 1 tablespoon salt and the fava beans and cook for 2 minutes. Reserve 1 cup of the cooking liquid and set aside. Drain the favas and immediately transfer them to the ice water to stop the cooking. Let sit in the water until cold, about 5 minutes. Drain well.

2. Transfer 1 cup of the favas to a food processor and pulse a few times to coarsely chop, then scrape them into a medium bowl. Add the remaining favas, the oil, lemon zest, and 2 tablespoons of the lemon juice to the food processor and season with salt and pepper. Process until smooth.

3. Add the fava purée to the bowl with the coarsely chopped favas. Fold in half the mint.

4. Spread some of the purée onto each slice of bread. Top with a few shavings of cheese and garnish with more mint before serving.

Crostini with Blue Cheese, Fig, Honey, and Hazelnuts

Makes 40 crostini

Figs and blue cheese are a classic Italian pairing. Since fig season is so short, I love using fig preserves, which is available all year round.

¼ cup **clover honey**

¼ teaspoon **coarsely ground black pepper**

8 ounces **Maytag blue cheese**, at room temperature

Perfect Crostini (page 71)

½ cup **fig preserves**

½ cup **hazelnuts**, toasted and coarsely chopped

1. In a small bowl, mix together the honey and pepper.

2. Put the blue cheese in a small bowl and mix with a wooden spoon until creamy.

3. Spread some of the cheese onto each crostini and top with a dollop of the fig preserves. Sprinkle with some of the nuts, drizzle with the honey, and serve.

Caramelized Onion and White Anchovy Egg Salad Crostini

Makes 40 crostini

There is a shop in Manhattan that does a sandwich with a soft-boiled egg, caramelized onions, and white anchovy on ciabatta bread. It's one of the best things I have ever eaten, and these crostini are an homage.

1 tablespoon **canola oil**

1 tablespoon **unsalted butter**

1 large **Vidalia onion**, halved and thinly sliced

Pinch of **sugar**

Kosher salt and **freshly ground black pepper**

8 **Perfect Hard-Cooked Eggs** (page 48), peeled

⅓ cup **crème fraîche**

1 teaspoon **Dijon mustard**

2 tablespoons finely chopped fresh **chervil**

Perfect Crostini (page 71)

20 **white anchovy fillets**, cut in half crosswise

1. Heat the oil and butter in a large sauté pan over medium heat until the butter has melted and the mixture begins to shimmer. Add the onion and sugar and cook, stirring occasionally, until golden brown and caramelized, about 30 minutes. Season with salt and pepper and set aside to cool.

2. Put 4 of the eggs in a food processor and pulse a few times to coarsely chop. Add the crème fraîche, mustard, ¼ teaspoon salt, and ¼ teaspoon pepper and process until smooth. Scrape into a medium bowl.

3. Finely chop the remaining 4 eggs on a cutting board and add them to the puréed egg mixture. Add the chervil and gently fold to combine. Taste and season with salt and pepper if needed.

4. Spread some of the caramelized onion on each crostini. Top each with a small dollop of the egg salad and half a white anchovy and serve.

NOTE White anchovies—*boquerones* when from Spain—are marinated in oil and vinegar and cold fresh. Tender white anchovies are cleaner tasting and milder than the oil- or salt-packed brown anchovies found on your grocery store shelf, and are a good introduction to the species for the anchovy-adverse.

Maple-Chile Glazed Mixed Nuts

After making your own glazed nuts, you will never be satisfied with the store-bought variety again. Preparing them yourself allows you to control the levels of sugar and spice, choose the nuts that you like (almonds, cashews, and pecans for me), and leave out the ones that you hate (see ya, Brazil nuts). Also, there is nothing like eating glazed nuts still warm from the oven, toasty and flavorful through and through. They're perfect served with a cocktail for an easy appetizer and will elevate any cheese-and-fruit plate to new heights. If you miraculously find yourself with leftovers, try chopping them and sprinkling them over yogurt or oatmeal for breakfast.

Serves 4 to 6

¼ cup **pure maple syrup**

1 tablespoon **light brown sugar**

1 **cinnamon stick**

2 **whole dried chiles de árbol**

Nonstick cooking spray

1 pound **mixed whole nuts**
(almonds, cashews, and pecans are my favorites)

1. Combine the maple syrup, brown sugar, cinnamon stick, and chiles in a small saucepan. Bring to a boil over high heat and cook, stirring once, until the sugar has dissolved. Remove the syrup from the heat, cover, and let steep at room temperature for at least 30 minutes and up to 24 hours. Discard the cinnamon stick and chiles before using.

2. Preheat the oven to 360°F. Lightly spray a nonstick baking sheet with nonstick spray or line it with a silicone baking mat.

3. Put the nuts in a large bowl, add the syrup, and mix using a rubber spatula until all the nuts are coated with the syrup. Spread the nuts into an even layer on the prepared baking sheet. Bake, tossing a few times, until golden brown and fragrant, about 12 minutes. Remove and let cool on the baking sheet. The nuts will keep in an airtight container in a cool, dark place for up to 5 days.

VEGETABLES + SIDES

You would never know it from reading the veggie-heavy menu at my restaurant Gato, but my menus used to be far more meat-centric—it's all a reflection of the times. For so many of us, vegetables used to be not just a "side," but an aside—an afterthought, something to round out the plate or throw together as a concession to the lone vegetarian in the party. Now we weigh our portions differently and embrace the delicious beauty that a plate of vegetables brings to the table for the betterment of all. I'm still down for a classic "meat and three" meal, but those three sides are more than supporting cast members. Today, dishes like Corn and Scallion Salad with Cilantro-Mint Dressing (page 89) get—and deserve—equal billing.

Caprese Salad The epitome of a summer salad, this must be made when tomatoes are at their peak. I don't deviate too far from the classic here, but rather expand upon its key elements. My caprese includes two types of mozzarella: milky, elastic fresh buffalo mozzarella, and decadent burrata, which is a pouch of fresh mozzarella filled with an almost fluid center of soft strings of cheese and cream. I also like to use a variety of tomatoes for different flavors and textures—this is the best time to hit up your farm stand for striped Green Zebras and Sungolds. There are a million reasons to love Italy's gorgeous Amalfi Coast, and this salad from the island of Capri might be one of the highest ranking reasons of all.

Serves 4 to 6

1 pint mixed **cherry tomatoes** (preferably heirloom), halved

7 tablespoons **extra-virgin olive oil**, plus more as needed

Flaky sea salt

2 pounds mixed medium and large **beefsteak tomatoes** (preferably heirloom), cut into thin slices

8 ounces fresh **buffalo** or **cow's-milk mozzarella cheese**, at room temperature, torn into pieces

8 ounces **burrata cheese**

Coarsely ground black pepper

Small **basil leaves**, for garnish

Grilled country bread, for serving (see Note)

NOTE To make the grilled bread, heat a grill to high. Grill 1-inch-thick slices of the bread on each side until lightly golden brown. Remove from the grill, brush the top with olive oil, and season with salt and pepper.

1. Put the cherry tomatoes in a large bowl with 2 tablespoons of the oil and season with salt. Toss to coat.

2. Arrange the tomato slices on a large platter or salad board, slightly overlapping; season generously with salt. Arrange the mozzarella over the tomatoes and tear the burrata into pieces over the top; lightly season with salt and pepper. Spoon the cherry tomatoes over the top, drizzle with the remaining 5 tablespoons oil, and season with pepper. Let stand for 30 minutes to let the flavors meld and the tomatoes and mozzarella release their juices.

3. Top the salad with basil and additional salt and oil, if desired. Serve with bread alongside.

Super Kale Salad with Peppadew Peppers, Cotija, and Crispy Pita

Super Kale Salad with Peppadew Peppers, Cotija, and Crispy Pita It has been years and kale is *still* the darling of the salad world. I'm not complaining. Actually, I'm glad, because raw or cooked, I'm all about kale. This salad has a lot going on: salty cotija cheese, piquant and sweet Peppadews, floral-tart Meyer lemon, crispy pita—it's got a great mix of textures and flavors, which is the key to a delicious salad.

Serves 4 to 6

2 medium bunches **lacinato kale** (dinosaur or Tuscan kale), ribs removed, leaves finely chopped (about 9 cups)

Meyer Lemon Vinaigrette (recipe follows)

8 ounces **cotija cheese**, coarsely grated

9 **Peppadew peppers**, drained and thinly sliced

2 large **scallions**, green and pale green parts only, thinly sliced

1 cup coarsely chopped store-bought or homemade **baked pita chips** (page 55)

1. Put the kale in a large bowl, add half the vinaigrette, and toss to coat. Let the kale sit at room temperature, tossing a few times, for at least 15 minutes and up to 30 minutes to soften it slightly.

2. Add the cheese, peppers, scallions, and remaining vinaigrette and toss to coat. Transfer to a large platter or shallow bowl. Top with the pita chips and serve.

Meyer Lemon Vinaigrette

Makes ¾ cup

¼ cup fresh **Meyer lemon juice** (see Tip)

¼ teaspoon **kosher salt**

⅛ teaspoon **freshly ground black pepper**

1 teaspoon **Dijon mustard**

1 teaspoon **clover honey**

½ cup **blended oil** (equal parts canola and extra-virgin olive oil)

Whisk together the lemon juice, salt, pepper, mustard, and honey in a medium bowl until the salt has dissolved. While whisking, slowly drizzle in the oil and whisk until emulsified. The vinaigrette can be made up to 1 day in advance and stored, tightly covered, in the refrigerator.

TIP Can't find Meyer lemons? Just use regular ones.

The Greek with Crispy Feta Croutons

Greek salad (or *horiatiki*, as it is known in Greece) is one of my all-time favorite salads. I love its bold combination of fresh, clean vegetables with salty, briny feta and olives and simple, acidic dressing. I honestly think I could eat it every day. In Greece, it's served without lettuce, but I like the American tradition of including it for some additional crunch and freshness. Crispy breaded cubes of feta are totally not classic, but they sure are delicious!

Serves 4 to 6

1 **red onion**, halved and thinly sliced

Red Wine Vinaigrette (recipe follows)

2 **English cucumbers**, halved and cut into 1-inch dice

1 pint **cherry tomatoes** (preferably heirloom), halved

Cherry beefsteak tomatoes, halved

1 cup **pitted kalamata olives**

1 cup fresh **flat-leaf parsley leaves**

1 head **romaine hearts**, thinly sliced

Crispy Feta Croutons (page 82)

1. Put the onion in a medium bowl, add the vinaigrette, and toss to coat. Let the onion marinate at room temperature for at least 15 minutes and up to 2 hours.

2. Put the cucumbers, tomatoes, olives, parsley, and romaine in a large bowl and toss to combine. Stir in the onions and vinaigrette and toss to coat.

3. Transfer the salad to a platter. Scatter the crispy feta over the top and serve.

Red Wine Vinaigrette

Makes about ¾ cup

3 tablespoons **red wine vinegar**

1 tablespoon fresh **lemon juice**

1 teaspoon **clover honey**

1 teaspoon **dried oregano**

¼ teaspoon **kosher salt**

⅛ teaspoon **freshly ground black pepper**

½ cup **blended oil** (equal parts canola and extra-virgin olive oil)

Whisk together the vinegar, lemon juice, honey, oregano, salt, and pepper in a medium bowl until the salt has dissolved. While whisking, slowly drizzle in the oil and whisk until emulsified. The vinaigrette can be made up to 1 day in advance and stored, tightly covered, in the refrigerator.

(recipe continues)

Crispy Feta Croutons

Makes 12 croutons

1 (6-ounce) block **Greek feta cheese**, drained and patted dry

1 cup **all-purpose flour**

Kosher salt and **freshly ground black pepper**

2 large **eggs**

1½ cups **panko bread crumbs**

1 cup **canola oil**

1. Cut the block of feta in half crosswise, then cut each half into 1-inch squares.

2. Spread the flour on a small plate and season with salt and pepper. Whisk together the eggs and 2 teaspoons water in a small shallow bowl. Place the panko in a separate shallow bowl.

3. Dredge the feta pieces in the flour and tap off any excess. Dip them into the egg mixture, letting any excess drip back into the bowl, then evenly coat the feta with the panko.

4. Line a baking sheet with paper towels and set it nearby. Heat the oil in a medium saucepan over medium heat until it begins to shimmer. (To test the oil, add a sprinkling of bread crumbs: if they sizzle, rise to the top, and turn golden brown, the oil is hot enough.) Working in batches, add the breaded feta cubes and cook until golden brown on both sides, about 2 minutes per side. Transfer to the paper towel–lined baking sheet and season lightly with salt. Repeat with the remaining feta. Eat immediately while warm.

Fried Green Tomatoes with Buffalo Mozzarella and Sweet-and-Sour Dressing

I fell in love with fried green tomatoes while traveling throughout the South for my show *Food Nation* many moons ago. This dish, a play on an Italian caprese made with fresh ripe red tomatoes, was on the inaugural menu at Bar Americain and often shows up at summer lunches at my house in the Hamptons.

Serves 3 or 4

1 cup **all-purpose flour**

2 cups **buttermilk**

2 cups **panko bread crumbs**

Kosher salt and **freshly ground black pepper**

3 large **green tomatoes**, sliced into ¼-inch-thick slices (you should have 12 pieces total)

2 cups **canola oil**

2 ounces **baby arugula**

Sweet-and-Sour Dressing (page 85)

1 pound **buffalo mozzarella cheese**, thinly sliced

2 **scallions**, green and light green parts only, thinly sliced

1. Put the flour in a shallow baking dish, the buttermilk in a second dish, and the panko in a third. Season each with salt and pepper.

2. Season the tomatoes on both sides with salt and pepper. Dredge the tomatoes in the flour and tap off any excess. Dip the tomatoes into the buttermilk and let the excess drip off, then dredge them in the panko, pressing the crumbs lightly to adhere.

3. Line a baking sheet with paper towels and set it nearby. Heat the oil in a large sauté pan over medium heat until it begins to shimmer. (To test the oil, add a sprinkling of bread crumbs: if they sizzle, rise to the top, and turn golden brown, the oil is hot enough.)

4. Working in batches of 3 or 4, fry the tomato slices in the hot oil until golden brown on both sides, about 2 minutes per side. Transfer the tomatoes to the paper towel–lined baking sheet and season with a bit more salt. Repeat with the remaining tomatoes.

5. Put the arugula in a large bowl, spoon some of the dressing around the bowl, and gently push the arugula into the dressing to evenly coat. Season with salt and pepper. Spread the arugula over a large platter and drizzle with a bit more dressing.

6. Arrange the fried green tomatoes on top of the arugula, slightly overlapping, and place the slices of cheese on top. Drizzle with a bit more dressing, garnish with the scallions, and serve.

(recipe continues)

Sweet-and-Sour Dressing

Makes about 1 cup

½ cup plus 2 tablespoons **canola oil**

2 **garlic cloves**, finely chopped to a paste with the side of a chef's knife and ¼ teaspoon kosher salt

1 tablespoon **tomato paste**

3 tablespoons **red wine vinegar**

1 tablespoon fresh **lemon juice**

1 tablespoon **ketchup**

2 teaspoons **Dijon mustard**

2 teaspoons **clover honey**

¼ teaspoon **kosher salt**

⅛ teaspoon **freshly ground black pepper**

1 large **scallion**, finely chopped

1. Heat 2 tablespoons of the oil in a small sauté pan over medium heat. Add the garlic and cook until soft, about 1 minute. Add the tomato paste and cook until the color deepens and the paste becomes fragrant, about 1 minute. Transfer to a medium bowl and let cool.

2. Add the vinegar, lemon juice, ketchup, mustard, honey, salt, and pepper to the bowl with the tomato paste and whisk until smooth. While whisking, slowly drizzle in the oil and whisk until emulsified, then fold in the scallion. Let sit at room temperature while you prepare the salad to allow the flavors to meld. The dressing can be made up to 1 day in advance and stored, tightly covered, in the refrigerator.

Harvest Salad with Apple Cider–Honey Vinaigrette

As soon as the air gets crisp and the days become shorter, I crave this salad. Asian pears, dried cranberries, wild rice, and walnuts come together and just scream "fall." Deep green kale is a gorgeous base for the ruby fruit and lightly golden nuts.

Serves 4 to 6

1 cup **wild rice**

Kosher salt

⅓ cup **dried cranberries**, soaked in warm water for 15 minutes and drained

1 bunch **lacinato kale** (dinosaur or Tuscan kale; about 1½ pounds), ribs removed, leaves coarsely chopped (about 8 cups)

4 ounces **baby spinach**, chopped

2 ripe **Asian pears**, halved, cored, and chopped

Apple Cider–Honey Vinaigrette (recipe follows)

Freshly ground black pepper

¾ cup **pecans** or **walnuts**, toasted and coarsely chopped

½ cup **pomegranate seeds**

1. Combine the rice, 4 cups cold water, and 2 teaspoons salt in a medium saucepan. Bring to a boil over high heat. Reduce the heat to low, cover, and cook until the rice has split (see Tip), about 1 hour. Drain the rice in a colander. Spread the rice over a baking sheet and let cool to room temperature.

2. Combine the cranberries, kale, spinach, pears, and cooled rice in a large bowl. Add half the vinaigrette and toss to coat, making sure everything is well coated. Season with salt and pepper.

3. Transfer the salad to a large shallow bowl or platter. Drizzle with the remaining vinaigrette, scatter the nuts and pomegranate seeds over the top, and serve.

TIP Wild rice should *not* be cooked to al dente, as it's best when allowed to bloom. I prefer mine slightly overcooked, until the grains are fully butterflied.

Apple Cider–Honey Vinaigrette

Makes about ¾ cup

1 cup **apple cider**

1 tablespoon finely diced **shallot**

2 teaspoons **cider vinegar**

1 teaspoon **Dijon mustard**

1 teaspoon **clover honey**

¼ teaspoon **kosher salt**

¼ teaspoon **freshly ground black pepper**

½ cup **blended oil** (equal parts canola and extra-virgin olive oil)

1. Put the apple cider in a small saucepan and bring to a boil over high heat. Cook until reduced to ¼ cup, about 10 minutes. Transfer to a medium heatproof bowl and let cool slightly.

2. Add the shallot, vinegar, mustard, honey, salt, and pepper and whisk until smooth. While whisking, slowly drizzle in the oil and whisk until emulsified. The vinaigrette can be made up to 8 hours in advance; whisk before using.

Corn and Scallion Salad with Cilantro-Mint Dressing

I pretty much live on the corn from Balsam Farms all summer while I'm in the Hamptons. My favorite way to eat it is steamed in the husk on the grill and slathered with a flavored butter and lots of salt. But sometimes you need a bit more refinement at your outdoor party, and during those times, this is how I love to serve it.

Serves 4

CILANTRO-MINT DRESSING

½ cup fresh **mint leaves**

¼ cup fresh **cilantro** or parsley leaves

¼ cup **white wine vinegar**

1 to 2 teaspoons **clover honey**

Kosher salt and **freshly ground black pepper**

¼ cup **olive** or **canola oil**

9 large ears **corn**, husks removed

Canola oil, for brushing

6 **scallions**, green and pale green parts only, thinly sliced

½ cup crumbled fresh **farmer's cheese** or feta cheese

1. **Make the dressing:** Combine the mint, cilantro, vinegar, 1 teaspoon of the honey, and salt and pepper to taste in a blender. Blend until smooth. With the motor running, slowly add the olive oil and blend until emulsified. Taste and add more honey, salt, and pepper as desired. Set aside.

2. Heat a grill to medium-high.

3. Brush the corn with some canola oil, then season with salt and pepper. Grill, covered, until lightly charred on all sides and tender, 2 to 3 minutes per side. Let cool slightly, then cut the corn kernels from the cobs and place them in a large bowl.

4. Add the scallions to the bowl and season with salt and pepper. Add some of the dressing and toss to coat. Top with the cheese and another drizzle of the dressing. Serve immediately.

NOTE If you don't have a grill, use a grill pan or boil the corn instead. Bring a large pot of salted water to a boil. Add the corn to the boiling water and cook until tender, 2 to 3 minutes, then drain.

Napa Slaw with Kimchi Vinaigrette

Napa Slaw with Kimchi Vinaigrette I love kimchi, a Korean side dish of salted and fermented vegetables seasoned with *lots* of garlic, scallion, and red chiles. It is not for the faint of heart (the smell alone can knock you off your feet), but trust me, it is amazing. Normally, it's eaten as a side dish, but it can also be incorporated into fried rice, pancakes, and noodle dishes for an intense punch of flavor. Here I use the base and some of its liquid to create a dressing for coleslaw (the perfect side for Korean BBQ Chicken, page 139). You may never go back to the mayonnaise version again.

Serves 4 to 6

½ cup prepared **kimchi**, plus
1 tablespoon juice from the jar

2 tablespoons **cider vinegar**

2 teaspoons **toasted sesame oil**

½ cup **canola oil**

2 teaspoons **clover honey**

1 medium head **napa cabbage**,
finely shredded

2 large **carrots**, coarsely grated

¼ cup fresh **cilantro leaves**

1 teaspoon **black sesame seeds**

1. Combine the kimchi, kimchi juice, vinegar, sesame oil, canola oil, and honey in a blender and blend until smooth and emulsified.

2. Combine the cabbage, carrots, and cilantro in a large bowl, add the dressing, and toss well to combine. Cover tightly and refrigerate for at least 1 hour and up to 8 hours before serving. Sprinkle with the sesame seeds when ready to serve.

Red Chile Caesar Salad with Cotija Frico Croutons

I served a version of this salad on my opening menu at Mesa Grill when it opened in New York City back in 1991. It was considered cutting edge at the time. Fast-forward twenty-seven years, and red chiles are in every grocery store and on countless menus in one form or another. Cotija is a crumbly Mexican cheese with a flavor like a cross between feta and Parmigiano Reggiano.

Serves 4 to 6

COTIJA FRICO

1 cup finely grated **cotija cheese**

1 teaspoon **all-purpose flour**

RED CHILE DRESSING

6 **anchovy fillets packed in oil**, drained and smashed to a paste

2 **garlic cloves**, chopped to a paste with the side of a chef's knife and ¼ teaspoon kosher salt

2 tablespoons prepared **mayonnaise**

1 tablespoon **Dijon mustard**

1 tablespoon **ancho chile powder**

2 teaspoons **puréed chipotle chile in adobo** (see Note, page 60)

Few dashes of **Worcestershire sauce**

Few dashes of **Tabasco sauce**

2 tablespoons **red wine vinegar**, or more to taste

Juice of 1 lime, or more to taste

Kosher salt and **freshly ground black pepper**

½ cup **olive oil**

2 **romaine hearts**, leaves separated and coarsely torn

1 head **red leaf lettuce**, coarsely torn

2 tablespoons chopped fresh **cilantro leaves**

1. Make the cotija frico. Preheat the oven to 425°F. Line a baking sheet with a silicone baking mat or parchment paper.

2. In a small bowl, combine the cheese and flour. Sprinkle 2 teaspoons of the mixture on the prepared baking sheet to form a 1-inch round. Spread the cheese evenly with a fork. Repeat with the rest of the cheese mixture, leaving 2 inches between each round. Bake until the fricos just begin to color, 6 to 8 minutes. Don't let them fully brown or the cheese will be bitter. Use a spatula to lift the edges of the fricos and loosen them from the pan; transfer to a separate baking sheet to cool.

3. Make the dressing: Combine the anchovy and garlic in a large bowl and mash together with a fork. Add the mayonnaise, mustard, ancho chile powder, chipotle purée, Worcestershire, Tabasco, vinegar, and lime juice and whisk until smooth. Season with ¼ teaspoon salt and ¼ teaspoon pepper. While whisking, slowly drizzle in the oil and whisk until emulsified. Taste and add a bit more vinegar, lime juice, or salt, if needed.

4. Put the romaine and red leaf lettuce in a large bowl. Spoon three-quarters of the dressing around the sides of the bowl and gently push the lettuces up into the dressing to lightly coat each leaf.

5. Transfer the lettuces to a large platter and drizzle with the remaining dressing. Garnish with the cilantro leaves and cotija frico and serve.

Spanish Panzanella with Horseradish Vinaigrette

Panzanella may be Tuscan in origin, and while I do cook a lot of Italian food at home, I make a lot of Spanish food, too. There's no reason the concept of bread salad can't travel across country lines, and that's what this version does. Membrillo, the sweet-tart Spanish quince paste, is a fantastic accompaniment to your cheese board, and you can usually find it in the gourmet cheese section of larger markets or in specialty cheese shops (and, of course, online). Bright and peppery, the horseradish-spiked vinaigrette provides a nice contrast to the sweet membrillo and slightly tangy and herbal Garrotxa, a semisoft goat cheese from northern Spain. If you can't find Garrotxa, Manchego is a perfectly acceptable substitute.

Serves 4 to 6

1 loaf **ciabatta**, cut into 1-inch cubes

¼ cup **olive oil**

Kosher salt and **freshly ground black pepper**

6 ounces **Garrotxa cheese**, grated

4 ounces **membrillo**, cut into small dice

2 ounces **baby arugula**

Horseradish Vinaigrette (recipe follows)

1. Preheat the oven to 350°F.

2. Put the bread in a large bowl, add the oil, and season with salt and pepper; toss to coat. Spread the bread on a baking sheet in a single layer. Bake until light golden brown, turning once, about 10 minutes.

3. Transfer the bread to a large bowl. Add the cheese, membrillo, arugula, and vinaigrette and toss well to coat. Transfer to a shallow bowl and let sit for about 15 minutes before serving.

Horseradish Vinaigrette

Makes about 1 cup

¼ cup **white wine vinegar**

1 tablespoon **Dijon mustard**

1½ teaspoons **clover honey**

Kosher salt and **freshly ground black pepper**

½ cup **blended oil** (equal parts canola and extra-virgin olive oil)

2 tablespoons prepared **horseradish**, drained

Whisk together the vinegar, mustard, honey, and salt and pepper to taste in a medium bowl. While whisking, slowly drizzle in the oil and whisk until emulsified. Just before serving, whisk in the horseradish. The vinaigrette can be made up to 8 hours in advance; whisk before using.

Roasted Sweet Potatoes with Spiced Tahini Honey

Anyone who knows me is well aware that I love sweet potatoes, autumnal spices, and honey—and this recipe combines them all. Instead of cutting the potatoes into perfect little cubes or chunks, I cut them into wedges that are big enough to pick up and eat with your hands. Mixing nutty tahini with sweet floral honey and warm cinnamon gives these potatoes a bit of a Middle Eastern touch. They're a great vegetable side dish to serve for Thanksgiving or Christmas, or even with a simple roast chicken or steak during the week.

Serves 4

SPICED TAHINI HONEY

½ cup best-quality **tahini**, stirred well

2 tablespoons **clover honey**

½ teaspoon **ground cinnamon**

1 teaspoon finely grated **orange zest**

3 large **sweet potatoes**, scrubbed

3 tablepoons **canola oil**

Kosher salt and **freshly ground black pepper**

1 heaping tablespoon **sesame seeds**, lightly toasted

1 large **green onion** (dark green and pale green parts), thinly sliced on the bias

1. Position a rack in the center of the oven and preheat the oven to 425°F.

2. Make the spiced tahini honey: Whisk together the tahini, honey, cinnamon, and orange zest in a small bowl until smooth. Cover and keep at room temperature while the potatoes roast.

3. Cut the potatoes in quarters, lengthwise, then cut each quarter in half crosswise into 2-inch-long pieces. Toss the potatoes with the oil on a rimmed baking sheet and season with salt and pepper. Roast, turning a few times, until golden brown and the flesh is soft when pierced with a knife, about 25 minutes.

4. Spread three-quarters of the sauce on a platter and top with the potatoes. Drizzle the remaining sauce on top and garnish with the sesame seeds and green onion.

Grilled Baby Eggplants with Fresh Ricotta and Farm Stand Tomatoes

This summery side is a staple at my summertime barbecues in the Hamptons, where it does double-duty as a substantial vegetarian offering. Baby eggplants are sweeter and more tender than the larger variety, and nothing is better than tomatoes at their peak. This dish can be easily adapted for the colder months, too: substitute a few teaspoons of chopped fresh oregano for the basil, use cherry tomatoes (they're great all year-round) instead of beefsteak, and, if your outdoor grill is off-limits after the first frost, cook the eggplants on a grill pan or in a preheated 400°F oven.

Serves 4

3 ripe large **beefsteak tomatoes**, halved, seeded, and diced

1 **garlic clove**, smashed

12 fresh **basil leaves**, thinly sliced

¼ cup chopped fresh **flat-leaf parsley leaves**

Kosher salt and **freshly ground black pepper**

1 cup fresh **whole-milk ricotta cheese**

1 teaspoon finely grated **lemon zest**

4 **baby eggplants**, halved

¼ cup **canola oil**

1. Combine the tomatoes, garlic, basil, and parsley in a large bowl and season with salt and pepper. Let sit at room temperature while you prepare the eggplant or for up to 2 hours.

2. Combine the ricotta and lemon zest in a small bowl and season with salt and pepper. Cover and refrigerate while you prepare the eggplant or for up to 2 hours.

3. Heat a grill to high or a grill pan over high heat.

4. Brush the eggplant on both sides with the canola oil and season with salt and pepper. Grill the eggplant, cut-side down, until golden brown and caramelized, about 4 minutes. Flip the eggplant and grill until the bottom is golden brown and the eggplant is tender, about 3 minutes more.

5. Transfer the eggplant to a platter, cut-side up, and top each half with a large dollop of the ricotta. Spoon the tomatoes over the top and serve.

End-of-Summer Tomato Soup

When I say "end-of-summer tomato soup," I really mean end of summer: when tomatoes are on their last leg (so to speak)—overly ripe and ready for the trash—is the peak moment for this soup. People always think I'm lying when I tell them how I make it—they're shocked that something this delicious has so few ingredients and that the base of the soup is water, not stock. Would I lie to you?

Serves 4 to 6

FRIED TORTILLAS (SEE NOTE)

Canola oil or peanut oil

2 **flour tortillas**, cut into long, thin strips

2 **corn tortillas**, cut into long, thin strips

Kosher salt

SOUP

2 tablespoons **olive oil**

1 medium **red onion**, coarsely chopped

2 **garlic cloves**, chopped

1 cup **dry white wine**

8 overly ripe **beefsteak tomatoes** (about 4 pounds total), seeded and coarsely chopped

¼ teaspoon **cayenne pepper**

Kosher salt and **freshly ground black pepper**

Grated white cheddar cheese

Diced avocado

Chopped fresh **cilantro**

1. **Make the fried tortillas:** Line a plate with paper towels and set it nearby. Fill a high-sided medium sauté pan with 1 inch of oil. Heat the oil over medium-high heat to 350°F (use a deep-fry thermometer). Working in batches, add the tortilla strips and fry until just crisp, 20 to 30 seconds. Using a slotted spoon, transfer the tortilla strips to the paper towel–lined plate and immediately season with salt.

2. **Make the soup:** Heat the olive oil in a medium saucepan over high heat. Add the onion and cook until soft, about 4 minutes. Add the garlic and cook for 30 seconds. Add the wine and cook until reduced by half. Add the tomatoes and enough water just to cover them. Bring to a boil, then reduce the heat to medium. Simmer until the tomatoes are very soft and starting to break down, about 30 minutes.

3. Working in batches, if needed, carefully transfer the mixture to a food processor and process until smooth. Return the mixture to the saucepan and season with the cayenne and salt and black pepper to taste. Bring to a simmer over high heat and cook for 5 minutes.

4. Ladle into bowls and garnish each with cheese, avocado, cilantro, and a few fried tortilla strips.

NOTE You can use store-bought fried or baked corn tortilla chips instead of making your own tortilla strips.

Sautéed Kale with Raisins and Pine Nuts

Southern Italians are enamored with pairing sweet and sour notes in their cooking (à la *agrodolce*), and I am in complete agreement. I find that the tangy contrast of red wine vinegar and sweet raisins plays especially well with the slightly bitter taste of the kale. If you aren't a fan of pine nuts, almonds work well, too.

Serves 4 to 6

½ cup **golden raisins**

½ cup **red wine vinegar**

3 tablespoons **sugar**

Kosher salt and **freshly ground black pepper**

Pinch of **Calabrian chile flakes**

2 tablespoons **canola oil**

1 medium **Spanish onion**, finely diced

1 pound **kale**, ribs removed, leaves coarsely chopped

¼ cup **pine nuts**

1. Bring 1½ cups water to a boil in a small saucepan over high heat. Put the raisins in a heatproof bowl, cover with the boiling water, and let the raisins soak until plump, about 15 minutes. Drain the raisins and return to the bowl.

2. Combine the vinegar and sugar in a small nonreactive saucepan and cook over high heat, stirring a few times, until the mixture has reduced by half and the sugar has melted, about 5 minutes. Add the vinegar mixture to the bowl with the raisins and toss to combine. Season with salt, pepper, and the chile flakes.

3. Heat the oil in a large high-sided sauté pan over high heat. Add the onion and cook, stirring occasionally, until lightly golden brown, about 5 minutes. Working in batches, add the kale and cook, stirring several times, until it begins to wilt, about 5 minutes. Add the raisin-vinegar mixture and cook until the kale is crisp-tender, about 5 minutes more. Stir in the pine nuts. Transfer to a large shallow bowl and serve.

Eleven-Layer Potato Gratin with Caramelized Shallots and Fried Sage

This potato gratin is seriously delicious. It first debuted on the menu at my Spanish-inspired restaurant, Bolo (which closed in 2007), as a side dish alongside roasted pork tenderloin with romesco sauce. Now it makes an appearance almost every Thanksgiving or Christmas, where it's served alongside my turkey or prime rib.

Serves 8

4 medium **Idaho** or **Russet potatoes**

2 cups **heavy cream**

Kosher salt and **freshly ground black pepper**

CARAMELIZED SHALLOTS

6 tablespoons (¾ stick) **unsalted butter**, cut into pieces

9 large **shallots**, sliced ¼ inch thick

Pinch of **sugar**

Kosher salt and **freshly ground black pepper**

FRIED SAGE LEAVES

1 cup **canola oil**

10 fresh **sage leaves**

Kosher salt

1. Preheat the oven to 375°F.

2. Peel the potatoes and thinly slice them (⅛ inch thick) on a mandoline. Place in a large bowl, cover with cold water, and let soak for at least 10 minutes and up to 4 hours. Drain well and pat dry.

3. Arrange a single layer of the potato slices over the bottom of a 10-inch square casserole or 3½-quart baking dish with 2-inch-high sides. Drizzle with 3 tablespoons of the cream and season with salt and pepper. Repeat with the remaining potatoes, cream, and salt and pepper to form eleven layers. Press down on the layers to totally submerge the potatoes in the cream mixture.

4. Cover with foil and bake for 30 minutes. Uncover and bake until the cream has been absorbed, the potatoes are cooked through, and the top is browned, 30 to 45 minutes more.

5. Make the caramelized shallots: While the gratin bakes, melt the butter in a large sauté pan over medium heat. Add the shallots and sugar and slowly cook, stirring occasionally, until golden brown and caramelized, about 40 minutes; season with salt and pepper. Set aside.

6. Make the fried sage leaves: Line a plate with paper towels and set it nearby. Heat the oil in a small saucepan over medium heat until it begins to shimmer. Working in batches, add the sage leaves and fry for a few seconds, until crisp. Using a slotted spoon, transfer the sage to the paper towel–lined plate and season with salt. (Let the sage-infused oil cool and save it to use for sautéing fish, chicken, or pork chops. It will keep in the refrigerator, tightly covered, for up to 1 month.)

7. Top the baked gratin with the caramelized shallots and fried sage leaves. Let rest for 10 minutes before slicing.

Roasted Button Mushrooms with Garlic-Parsley Butter

Sautéed mushrooms were a constant on the menu of just about every steakhouse in the 1970s, and you better believe they were plain old white button mushrooms and not some fancy variety, either. But here's the thing: they were delicious. Button mushrooms don't get the respect that they deserve these days, so let's throw it back and see that they do. Butter, garlic, wine, and parsley—you can tell right off the bat that this dish is going to be a good thing. Don't toss out the mushroom stems: store them in a zip-top plastic storage bag in the freezer to use for a mushroom stock or soup.

Serves 4 to 6

GARLIC-PARSLEY BUTTER

½ cup (1 stick) **unsalted butter**, at room temperature

3 **garlic cloves**, chopped to a paste with the side of a chef's knife and ¼ teaspoon kosher salt

¼ cup finely chopped fresh **flat-leaf parsley leaves**

1 tablespoon **dry white wine**

Kosher salt and **freshly ground black pepper**

1½ pounds **button mushrooms**, washed and stemmed (see headnote)

3 tablespoons **canola oil**

Kosher salt and **freshly ground black pepper**

¼ cup chopped fresh **flat-leaf parsley leaves**

1. **Make the garlic-parsley butter:** Combine the butter, garlic, parsley, and wine in a small bowl and season with salt and pepper. Cover and refrigerate for at least 30 minutes and up to 24 hours to allow the flavors to meld before using.

2. Preheat the oven to 425°F.

3. Toss the mushroom caps with the oil in a large bowl and season with salt and pepper. Transfer to a large cast-iron pan or *cazuela* and roast until golden brown and soft, turning once, about 25 minutes. Remove the pan from the oven. Add the garlic-parsley butter, return the pan to the oven, and roast, stirring once, until the butter has melted and coated the mushrooms, about 5 minutes. Remove from the oven.

4. Stir in the parsley and serve the mushrooms directly from the pan.

Crispy Coconut-Scallion Rice

If there is one single dish that is responsible for me winning on *Beat Bobby Flay*, it is this one. Not served on its own, obviously, but alongside braises and Asian-inspired dishes. If the judges were tied on their decision, this coconut rice, with its crispy bottom, was the deciding factor. It should come as no surprise that it is just as popular when I serve it at home. If you can make the rice the night before or use leftover rice from Chinese takeout, all the better. The rice really needs to be cool and separated to get really crispy—it will not work with warm rice.

Serves 4

1 cup unsweetened full-fat canned **coconut milk**

Kosher salt and **freshly ground black pepper**

2 cups **Carolina long-grain rice**

½ cup thinly sliced **scallions**, plus more for garnish

¼ cup **canola oil**

1. Combine the coconut milk, 2 teaspoons salt, ¼ teaspoon pepper, and 1 cup water in a medium saucepan and bring to a boil over high heat. Stir in the rice and bring back to a boil. Reduce the heat to medium-low, cover, and cook until the liquid has been absorbed and the rice is tender, about 18 minutes.

2. Remove the pan from the heat and let sit, covered, for 5 minutes. Remove the lid and fluff the rice with a fork. Spread the rice in an even layer over a large baking sheet and let cool completely, about 30 minutes. The rice can be made up to 24 hours in advance; store it on the baking sheet, covered with plastic wrap, in the refrigerator.

3. Combine the rice and scallions in a large bowl. Heat the oil in a large cast-iron or nonstick pan over high heat until it begins to shimmer. Add the rice and, using a heavy-duty metal spatula, immediately press the rice down into the pan until the top is flat. Cook, without stirring, until the bottom becomes golden brown and crispy, about 5 minutes (start checking at 4 minutes, making sure not to burn it). Turn the rice over and press down firmly on the top again. Cook until the bottom is golden brown and crispy, about 5 minutes more. Transfer to a platter, sprinkle with more scallions, and serve.

Mashed Potatoes with Green Chile Queso Sauce

Each year for Thanksgiving, I create a theme for the meal. Some of my past dinners have been Spanish, Italian (yes, I know it is an American holiday, but hey, we all came from somewhere, right?), but also New England, the Pacific Northwest, and, of course, the Southwest. These mashed potatoes, served with a pool of creamy, peppery queso in the center, made their debut (to great fanfare, it must be said) at just such a meal.

Serves 4 to 6

3 pounds **Yukon Gold potatoes**, peeled and cut into 2-inch dice

Kosher salt

2 cups **whole milk**

½ cup (1 stick) **unsalted butter**, cut into pieces

2 tablespoons **all-purpose flour**

1 cup packed grated **Monterey Jack cheese**

¼ cup freshly grated **Parmigiano Reggiano cheese**

1 large **poblano chile**, roasted, peeled, seeded, and finely diced (see Tip; page 54)

¼ cup finely chopped fresh **cilantro leaves**, plus more for garnish

Freshly ground black pepper

1 cup **heavy cream**

1. Put the potatoes in a large pot with 2 tablespoons salt and cover with cold water by a few inches. Bring to a boil over high heat, cover, and cook until a paring knife inserted into a potato meets no resistance, about 25 minutes.

2. Put the milk in a small saucepan and bring to a simmer over low heat.

3. Meanwhile, melt 2 tablespoons of the butter in a medium saucepan over medium heat. Whisk in the flour and cook until the mixture is smooth and pale, 1 minute. Whisk in the hot milk and increase the heat to high. Cook, whisking frequently, until the milk has thickened and the raw flour taste has been cooked out, about 5 minutes. Remove from the heat and whisk in the Monterey Jack cheese until smooth and melted. Stir in the Parmigiano Reggiano, the poblano, and cilantro. Season with salt and pepper and keep warm.

4. Drain the potatoes well and return them to the pot. Heat over low heat to dry them out. Combine the cream and remaining 6 tablespoons (¾ stick) butter in a small saucepan and heat over low heat until the butter has melted, about 5 minutes.

5. When the potatoes turn white and become dry, pass them through a ricer into a large glass bowl. Using a wooden spoon, gently combine the potatoes with the warm cream-butter mixture. Season with salt and pepper.

6. Transfer the potatoes to a large shallow bowl. Make a well in the middle of the potatoes and fill with the cheese sauce. Garnish with the cilantro and serve.

Cranberries with Campari and Grapefruit

Speaking of an Italian Thanksgiving, I served this for Thanksgiving dinner in 2012, when the theme that year was Southern Italy. Forget the canned stuff—homemade cranberry relish is so easy and can be made several days ahead. Campari is an Italian aperitif with a bitter flavor that echoes the bitter grapefruit and balances the tart cranberries. If you aren't a fan of grapefruit, any citrus will work (some of my favorites are tangerine, clementine, and kumquat).

Serves 6 to 8

2 tablespoons **canola oil**

1 small **red onion**, finely diced

2 tablespoons finely grated fresh **ginger**

1 cup fresh **orange juice**

1 cup fresh **Texas Red grapefruit juice**

¾ cup **pure cane sugar**, plus more if needed

1 pound fresh or frozen **cranberries** (not thawed if frozen)

2 tablespoons **Campari**

2 **Texas Red grapefruits**, segmented

2 teaspoons finely grated **orange zest**

Kosher salt and **freshly ground black pepper**

Chopped fresh **flat-leaf parsley leaves**, for garnish

1. Heat the oil in a medium saucepan over medium heat. Add the onion and ginger and cook until the onion is soft, about 5 minutes. Add the orange juice, grapefruit juice, and sugar and bring to a boil. Cook until the sugar has melted and the mixture has reduced slightly, about 8 minutes.

2. Stir in half the cranberries and cook, stirring occasionally, until the berries pop and break down and the mixture begins to thicken, about 10 minutes. Add the remaining cranberries and the Campari and cook just until the berries pop, about 5 minutes.

3. Remove from the heat, stir in the grapefruit segments and orange zest, and season lightly with salt and pepper. Transfer to a bowl, stir in the parsley, and serve at room temperature. The relish can be made up to 2 days in advance and served cold or at room temperature.

PIZZA + PASTA

I've made a public declaration of my love for Italy: the culture, architecture, the fusion of modern style and ancient history, and . . . the pizza and pasta. Who doesn't love Italian food?! I challenge you to present your family table with a bowl of richly satisfying Eggplant Bolognese (page 125) and not give into your inner *nonna,* saying "Mangia, mangia!" as you ladle out first and second helpings. The NYC pizzeria where I had my first job as a delivery boy may no longer be open, but that kid who would work for a 25-cent tip and a free slice of pizza? He's still in business. These days, I am lucky enough to have a real-deal pizza oven at my house in the Hamptons where I turn out seasonally inspired pizzas to hungry crowds every weekend. You don't need a professional oven to pull off great pizza at home, however—just a recipe for perfect pizza dough (see page 112). I got mine from a pro and am more than happy to share.

My Favorite Homemade Pizza Dough

This is perfect pizza dough. I'm not bragging, because it's the truth. While I would love to take credit for the recipe, I owe my thanks to the great chef who shared it with me, Chris Bianco. Chris gave me his permission to use it more than ten years ago, and I am forever grateful. I have a pizza oven at my home in the Hamptons and I make pizza all summer for breakfast, lunch, and dinner—I never met a meal I didn't want on a pizza. If you don't have a pizza oven, just turn up your oven as high as it goes and invest in a pizza stone for great results.

Makes enough dough for four 14-inch personal pizzas

2 cups **warm water** (105°F to 115°F)

1 (¼-ounce) package **active dry yeast** (2¼ teaspoons)

5 to 5½ cups **unbleached all-purpose flour** (preferably organic), plus more for dusting

2 teaspoons **fine sea salt**

Extra-virgin olive oil

1. Put the warm water in a large bowl and add the yeast. Let stand for 5 minutes. Stir in 3 cups of the flour and the salt and stir until smooth. Stir in an additional 2 cups flour; continue adding flour, 1 tablespoon at a time (up to ½ cup more), until the dough comes away from the bowl but is still sticky.

2. Turn the dough out onto a lightly floured work surface and knead it with lightly floured hands. Start by slapping the dough onto the counter, pulling it toward you with one hand and pushing it away from you with the other. Fold the dough back over itself (use a bench scraper or a wide knife to help scrape the dough from the work surface). Repeat until it's easier to handle, about 10 times. Finish kneading normally until the dough is smooth, elastic, and soft but still a little tacky, about 10 minutes.

3. Shape the dough into a ball and transfer it to a bowl lightly coated with olive oil; turn to coat with the oil. Cover with plastic wrap and let the dough rise in a warm place until it doubles in volume, about 3 hours. Press it with your finger: if it's done, an indentation should remain.

4. Scrape the dough out of the bowl onto a floured surface and cut it into 4 pieces. Shape each piece into a ball. Dust with flour and cover with plastic wrap. Let rest for at least 20 minutes and up to 45 minutes, allowing the dough to relax and almost double in size. Gently roll the dough out on a lightly floured surface and stretch it with your hands, then top and bake as directed in the recipe (see pages 113, 116, and 118).

Pizza Margherita Probably the most classic of Italy's pizza, the Margherita has just three toppings: tomato sauce, mozzarella cheese, and basil (or it would, except that I add a few chile flakes for a touch of heat, and some grated Parm, so five). A vital element in creating a perfect pie is to not overload it with toppings. You'll end up with a soggy crust if you do, and nobody likes that. I like to say that more isn't better, it's just more.

Makes four 14-inch personal pizzas

My Favorite Homemade Pizza Dough (page 112)

Coarse **cornmeal**

Extra-virgin olive oil

Kosher salt and **freshly ground black pepper**

2 cups **Marinara Sauce** (page 126) or your favorite store-bought marinara

12 ounces fresh **mozzarella cheese**, thinly sliced

Calabrian chile flakes

Freshly grated **Parmigiano Reggiano cheese** (optional)

24 fresh **basil leaves**, torn

1. Put a pizza stone on the bottom rack of the oven and preheat the oven to 500°F for at least 30 minutes.

2. On a lightly floured surface, roll or stretch one ball of pizza dough into a 14-inch round. Sprinkle cornmeal onto a pizza peel, an unrimmed baking sheet, or a rimmed baking sheet turned upside down. Transfer the dough to the peel or baking sheet. (Alternatively, sprinkle cornmeal onto parchment paper, place the dough on top of the paper, then transfer the topped dough on the paper to the baking stone.)

3. Brush the dough with a few teaspoons of oil and season with salt and pepper. Spread ½ cup of the sauce evenly over the top of the dough, leaving a 1-inch border. Arrange one-quarter of the cheese over the sauce and sprinkle with chile flakes. Slide the pizza onto the pizza stone. Bake until the crust is golden brown on top and bottom, about 12 minutes. Remove from the oven. Sprinkle Parmigiano over the top and add one-quarter of the basil. Drizzle with a bit more oil. Let sit for 2 minutes before slicing. Repeat with the remaining dough and toppings to make three additional pizzas.

Variations

Green Olive, Capers, and Basil Add ½ cup thinly sliced pitted Picholine olives and 1 tablespoon drained capers on top of the marinara sauce before adding the cheese.

Pepperoni and Calabrian Honey Add 16 thin slices pepperoni on top of the marinara sauce before adding the cheese. Bake as directed. Remove from the oven and drizzle with honey and sprinkle with a pinch of Calabrian chile flakes.

**Pizza
Margherita, page 113**

Pizza with Green Tomato, Scallion Pesto, and Asparagus, page 116

Pizza with Green Tomato, Scallion Pesto, and Asparagus

I love spring—first, because our winters on the East Coast seem to be colder and snowier than ever before, and second, because I love spring vegetables. I say good-bye to the earthy-colored vegetables of fall and winter, with their long roasting times, and hello to all things green, fresh, and quick cooking. This pizza screams "spring and summer," and it is always on the menu for my first pool party of the season.

Makes four 14-inch personal pizzas

GRILLED ASPARAGUS

12 **asparagus spears**, trimmed

2 tablespoons **canola oil**

Kosher salt and **freshly ground black pepper**

My Favorite Homemade Pizza Dough (page 112)

Coarse **cornmeal**

Extra-virgin olive oil

Kosher salt and **freshly ground black pepper**

Green Tomato Sauce (recipe follows)

8 ounces **whole-milk mozzarella cheese**, coarsely grated

1 pound **fresh mozzarella cheese**, torn into 12 pieces

¼ cup freshly grated **Parmigiano Reggiano cheese**

½ cup **Scallion Pesto** (page 243)

Finely grated **zest of 1 fresh lemon**

¼ cup sliced **Pickled Chiles** (serrano, jalapeño, or Fresno; page 249), drained

1. Put a pizza stone on the bottom rack of the oven and preheat the oven to 500°F for at least 30 minutes.

2. Heat a grill to high or heat a grill pan over high heat. Brush the asparagus with the oil and season with salt and pepper. Grill on both sides until golden brown, charred, and just cooked through, about 1 minute per side. Transfer the asparagus to a cutting board and cut each piece into thirds.

3. On a lightly floured surface, roll or stretch one ball of pizza dough into a 14-inch round. Sprinkle cornmeal onto a pizza peel, an unrimmed baking sheet, or a rimmed baking sheet turned upside down. Transfer the dough onto the peel or baking sheet. (Alternatively, sprinkle cornmeal onto parchment paper, place the dough on top of the paper, then transfer the dough on the paper to the baking stone.)

4. Brush the dough with a few teaspoons of oil and season with salt and pepper. Spread ⅓ cup of the sauce evenly over the top of the dough, leaving a 1-inch border. Spread one-quarter of the grated mozzarella over the sauce. Place one-quarter of the asparagus over the cheese. Scatter one-quarter of the torn mozzarella over the top. Slide onto the pizza stone. Bake until the crust is golden brown on top and bottom, about 12 minutes. Remove from the oven and sprinkle 1 tablespoon of the Parmigiano Reggiano cheese over the top. Drizzle with 2 tablespoons of the pesto and garnish with one-quarter of the lemon zest and 1 tablespoon of the chiles. Let sit for 2 minutes before slicing and serving. Repeat with the remaining dough and toppings to make three additional pizzas.

Green Tomato Sauce

Makes 1½ cups

2 tablespoons **olive oil**

½ small **Spanish onion**, finely diced

2 **garlic cloves**, finely chopped

2½ pounds **green tomatoes**, cored and chopped, or tomatillos, husked, scrubbed, and chopped

Kosher salt and **freshly ground black pepper**

¼ cup chopped fresh **cilantro**, parsley, or basil

1. Heat the oil in a medium saucepan over medium heat. Add the onion and cook until soft, about 5 minutes. Add the garlic and cook until soft, about 1 minute.

2. Add the tomatoes and ¼ cup water and bring to a boil. Reduce the heat to medium and cook, stirring occasionally, until the tomatoes release their juices and completely break down, about 10 minutes. Carefully transfer the mixture to a blender or food processor and blend until smooth. Return the mixture to the pan and bring to a boil over high heat. Reduce the heat to low and cook until the sauce thickens and has reduced to about 1½ cups. Season with salt and pepper, remove from the heat, and fold in the herb. The sauce can be made up to 3 days in advance and stored, tightly covered, in the refrigerator.

Lamb Sausage Pizza with Manchego and Mint Pesto

This is one of the first pizzas I created for my menu at Gato, and I make it for friends all summer in the Hamptons. Merguez is a highly spiced North African lamb sausage with a good amount of heat, courtesy of harissa and cayenne. Manchego, a slightly piquant sheep's-milk cheese from Spain, is one of my all-time favorites. Mint pesto adds a touch of freshness to this earthy pizza, and, of course, lamb and mint is such a classic pairing.

Makes four 14-inch personal pizzas

My Favorite Homemade Pizza Dough (page 112)

Coarse **cornmeal**

Extra-virgin olive oil

Kosher salt and **freshly ground black pepper**

2 cups **Marinara Sauce** (page 126) or your favorite store-bought marinara sauce

1 pound **uncooked merguez sausage**, thinly sliced

12 ounces **Manchego cheese**, coarsely grated

½ cup freshly grated **Parmigiano Reggiano**

Mint Pesto (recipe follows)

1. Put a pizza stone on the bottom rack of the oven and preheat the oven to 500°F for at least 30 minutes.

2. On a lightly floured surface, roll or stretch one ball of pizza dough into a 14-inch round. Sprinkle cornmeal onto a pizza peel, an unrimmed baking sheet, or a rimmed baking sheet turned upside down. Transfer the dough to the peel or baking sheet. (Alternatively, sprinkle cornmeal onto parchment paper, place the dough on top of the paper, then transfer the dough on the paper to the baking stone.)

3. Brush the dough with a few teaspoons of oil and season with salt and pepper. Spread ½ cup of the sauce evenly over the dough, leaving a 1-inch border. Arrange one-quarter of the sausage over the sauce. Sprinkle one-quarter of the Manchego cheese over the lamb. Slide the pizza onto the pizza stone. Bake until the crust is golden brown on top and bottom, about 12 minutes. Remove from the oven. Sprinkle 2 tablespoons of the Parmigiano Reggiano over the top and drizzle with 2 tablespoons of the pesto. Drizzle with a bit more oil. Let sit for 2 minutes before slicing and serving. Repeat with the remaining dough and toppings to make three additional pizzas.

Mint Pesto

Makes about ½ cup

¼ cup tightly packed fresh
mint leaves

¼ cup tightly packed fresh **flat-leaf
parsley leaves**

1 **garlic clove**, chopped

2 tablespoons **pine nuts**

¼ cup **extra-virgin olive oil**

2 tablespoons finely grated
Parmigiano Reggiano cheese

Kosher salt and **freshly ground
black pepper**

Combine the herbs, garlic, and pine nuts in a small food processor and pulse to coarsely chop. Add the oil and process until smooth. If the mixture is too thick, add a bit more oil to loosen it. Add the cheese and salt and pepper to taste. Process to combine and scrape into a bowl. The pesto can be made up to 3 days in advance and stored, tightly covered, in the refrigerator.

Homemade Fresh Pasta
This is my tried-and-true pasta recipe—when you find something that works for you, stick with it. I'm sticking with this pasta, using it for everything from spaghetti to linguine, lasagna to ravioli.

Makes about 1½ pounds pasta

2 cups **all-purpose flour**, plus more for dusting

3 large **eggs**

1 large **egg yolk**

1. Combine the flour, eggs, and egg yolk in a food processor and pulse until a dough comes together. Transfer to a counter dusted lightly with flour and knead gently until the dough comes together and is smooth, about 1 minute. Wrap in plastic wrap and refrigerate for at least 30 minutes and up to 24 hours.

2. Divide the dough into 4 pieces. With your hands, flatten and shape one piece of dough into a ½-inch-thick rectangle. Dust it lightly with flour and pass it through a pasta machine on the thickest setting. If the dough comes out oddly shaped, re-form into a rectangle. Fold it in thirds, like a letter, and, if necessary, flatten it to ½-inch thickness. Pass it through the pasta machine on the thickest setting again, with the seam of the letter perpendicular to the rollers. Repeat this folding-and-rolling step 10 to 12 times, dusting the dough with flour if it becomes sticky.

3. Without folding the dough, pass it through the pasta machine on the next thinnest setting. Keep reducing the space between the rollers after each pass, lightly dusting the pasta with flour on both sides each time, until the pasta sheet is about 1/16 inch thick.

4. Lay the sheet of rolled-out dough on a counter and cover with a dish towel. Roll out the remaining dough. Cut each sheet into 11-inch lengths. Use a sharp knife to cut the dough into your desired noodle shape (fettuccine, pappardelle, etc.). (Alternatively, if you have a cutting attachment on your pasta maker, use that.)

5. Cook the pasta in boiling salted water until it rises to the top of the water, about 3 to 4 minutes. If you're not cooking the pasta right away, let it dry on a baking sheet for 1 to 2 minutes, dust well with flour so the strands will not stick together, and loosely fold them or form them into small nests. Let dry for about 30 minutes more, then wrap in plastic wrap and store in the refrigerator for up to 2 days.

Variations

Black Squid Ink Pasta Add 1 tablespoon squid ink to the eggs and whisk until combined.

Smoked Paprika Pasta Add 1 tablespoon sweet smoked paprika to the flour.

Saffron Pasta Add 1 tablespoon ground saffron to the eggs. Whisk to combine and let bloom for 5 minutes.

Quick Bolognese Sauce

This is the quick Bolognese sauce that I made on an episode of *Beat Bobby Flay*—it had to be both really good *and* really fast. It is not the long-simmering version that you'd find in Bologna, but it's delicious in its own right.

Makes about 6 cups

MEAT

2 tablespoons **olive oil**

8 ounces **bacon**, diced

1½ pounds **80% lean ground chuck**

½ pound **80% lean ground pork**

1 teaspoon **ground fennel**

¼ teaspoon **Calabrian chile flakes**

Kosher salt and **freshly ground black pepper**

SAUCE

2 tablespoons **olive oil**

1 medium **red onion**, finely diced

½ medium **carrot**, finely diced

1 medium **celery stalk**, finely diced

1 small **fennel bulb**, finely diced

4 **garlic cloves**, finely chopped to a paste using the side of a chef's knife and ¼ teaspoon kosher salt

2 tablespoons **tomato paste**

1 teaspoon **ground fennel**

1 cup **rosé wine**

1 (28-ounce) can **plum tomatoes** and their juices

2 cups **chicken stock**

Kosher salt and **freshly ground black pepper**

¼ cup chopped fresh **flat-leaf parsley leaves**, plus more for garnish

1 tablespoon finely chopped fresh **oregano**

1. Cook the meat: Line a plate with paper towels and set it nearby. Heat the oil in a large Dutch oven over medium heat. Add the bacon and cook slowly until the fat has rendered and the bacon is crisp, about 5 minutes. Remove with a slotted spoon and transfer to the paper towel–lined plate to drain.

2. Increase the heat to high, add the beef and pork to the pan, and season with the ground fennel, chile flakes, and salt and pepper to taste. Cook, stirring occasionally, until golden brown, about 10 minutes. Drain the excess fat from the pot and set the meat aside.

3. Make the sauce: Add the oil to the Dutch oven over medium-high heat and heat until it begins to shimmer. Add the onion, carrot, celery, and diced fennel and cook until soft, about 5 minutes. Add the garlic and cook for 1 minute. Add the tomato paste and ground fennel and cook for 1 minute more.

4. Add the wine and cook until reduced by half, about 3 minutes. Add the tomatoes and stock and cook until the tomatoes begin to soften, about 10 minutes. Using a potato masher or wooden spoon, coarsely mash the tomatoes. Season with salt and pepper and cook until the sauce comes to a boil and begins to thicken slightly, about 15 minutes. Add the meat to the pan and cook until the sauce thickens and combines, about 20 minutes more. Remove from the heat. Fold in the parsley and oregano and season with salt and pepper. Use immediately, or let cool to room temperature, transfer to an airtight container, and store in the refrigerator for up to 3 days or in the freezer for up to 1 month.

Eggplant Bolognese

This meaty but meatless wonder is sure to thrill the vegetarians among your friends and family, and it's just as satisfying to those who check the carnivore box. My pasta of choice for this dish is tortiglioni (a large, tube-shaped noodle with deep spiral grooves), but any version of rigatoni and fettuccine will work.

Serves 4 to 6

6 **baby eggplants**, or 1 large globe eggplant

½ cup **olive oil**

Kosher salt and **freshly ground black pepper**

1 large **Spanish onion**, finely diced

2 medium **carrots**, finely diced

1 small **celery stalk**, finely diced

4 **garlic cloves**, finely chopped to a paste with the side of a chef's knife and ¼ teaspoon kosher salt

¼ to ½ teaspoon **Calabrian chile flakes**, depending on how spicy you like it

1 cup **dry red wine**

2 (28-ounce) cans **plum tomatoes**, with their juices

1 teaspoon **sugar**

¼ cup chopped fresh **basil leaves**

2 tablespoons finely chopped fresh **oregano**

1. Preheat the oven to 350°F.

2. Peel half the skin from the eggplants in 1-inch sections (so the eggplant looks striped). Slice each eggplant crosswise into ¼-inch thick rounds and cut each round into ½-inch dice.

3. Heat 3 tablespoons of the oil in a large sauté pan over high heat until it begins to shimmer. Add half the eggplant, season with salt and pepper, and cook, stirring continuously, until the eggplant takes on some color and becomes soft, about 5 minutes. Spread the eggplant on a baking sheet in an even layer. Add 3 tablespoons of the oil to the pan and repeat with the remaining eggplant.

4. Transfer the eggplant to the oven and bake until very soft, turning once, about 15 minutes. Remove from the oven and let cool.

5. Heat the remaining 2 tablespoons oil in a Dutch oven over high heat. Add the onion, carrots, and celery and cook, stirring often, until soft, about 5 minutes. Add the garlic and cook for 30 seconds. Add the chile flakes and cook for 30 seconds more.

6. Stir in the wine and bring to a boil. Cook until the liquid has completely reduced, about 5 minutes. Add the tomatoes with their juices and the sugar and bring to a boil. Reduce the heat to medium and cook until the tomatoes begin to soften and break down, about 15 minutes. Using a potato masher, coarsely mash the tomatoes and cook, stirring occasionally, until the sauce has thickened, about 20 minutes more.

7. Fold the eggplant, basil, and oregano into the sauce. Season with salt and pepper. Use immediately, or let cool to room temperature, transfer to an airtight container, and store in the refrigerator for up to 3 days or in the freezer for up to 1 month.

Marinara Sauce

I didn't have an Italian mother or grandmother, but when you grew up in Manhattan in the '70s, marinara sauce (or "gravy") was part of your life. If I wasn't eating it at my Italian friend's house for dinner, then my grandfather was taking me to Little Italy for a big plate of spaghetti and meatballs. My marinara proves that you don't have to be Italian to make a really good red sauce. Growing up as I did in a city with such a rich Italian American culture, eating all those Italian Sunday dinners in home kitchens or restaurants, I'd like to think that I know what good marinara sauce should taste like. In my opinion, it should taste like this. Something out of a jar? Fuggedaboutit!

Makes 6 cups

2 tablespoons **olive oil**

1 medium **Spanish onion**, finely chopped

4 **garlic cloves**, finely chopped

⅛ to ¼ teaspoon **crushed red pepper flakes**, depending on how spicy you like it

2 tablespoons **tomato paste**

2 (28-ounce) cans **plum tomatoes**, with their juices

¼ cup chopped **flat-leaf parsley leaves**

1 tablespoon finely chopped fresh **oregano**

Kosher salt and **freshly ground black pepper**

¼ cup chopped fresh **basil leaves**

1. Heat the oil in a large saucepan over medium-high heat. Add the onion and cook until soft, about 5 minutes. Add the garlic and red pepper flakes and cook for 1 minute. Add the tomato paste and cook until it deepens slightly in color, about 1 minute.

2. Stir in the tomatoes and their juices. Rinse each can with ¼ cup water and add the water to the pot. Bring to a boil over high heat. Reduce the heat to medium and cook until the tomatoes become very soft and begin to break down, about 15 minutes. Using a potato masher, mash the tomatoes into a coarse purée. Add the parsley and oregano and cook, stirring occasionally, until the sauce has thickened, about 20 minutes. Season with salt and black pepper and stir in the basil.

3. Use immediately, or let cool completely and store in an airtight container in the refrigerator for up to 3 days or in the freezer for up to 1 month.

NOTE Make a double batch and store the extra sauce in the freezer. That way, any time you want a plate of spaghetti with marinara or a good base for a Pizza Margherita (page 113), you've got it at the ready.

Calabrian Chile Crab Spaghetti with Garlic Bread Crumbs

Every year, my good friend Jimmy ("JimmyV") Ventura sends 60 pounds of stone crab claws to the office in celebration of Crabsgiving, our favorite fictional holiday that lands some time in the week before Thanksgiving. (This is how we do "Friendsgiving," thanks to Jimmy.) Now, the best way to eat stone crab claws is steamed and dipped in mustard sauce, but when you're looking at 60 pounds of them, you need to get creative. Imagine if Forrest Gump went crabbing instead of shrimping: we do crab cakes, crab salads, crab dips, and more. My contribution is always this lemony, garlic-and-Calabrian-chile-spiked pasta dish. I make this when it's not Crabsgiving, too, forgoing the flown-in-from-Florida stone crab for Maryland jumbo lump blue crab.

Serves 4 to 6

Kosher salt

1 pound **dried spaghetti**

¼ cup **extra-virgin olive oil**

6 **garlic cloves**, finely chopped to a paste with the side of a chef's knife and ¼ teaspoon kosher salt

¼ to ½ teaspoon **Calabrian chile flakes** (depending on how spicy you like it)

6 **anchovy fillets packed in oil**, drained and finely chopped

1 cup **dry white wine**

½ cup (1 stick) cold **unsalted butter**, cut into pieces

1 pound **jumbo lump crabmeat**, picked over

¼ cup chopped fresh **flat-leaf parsley leaves**, plus more for garnish (optional)

Finely grated **zest of 2 lemons**, plus more for garnish

Freshly ground black pepper

Garlic Bread Crumbs (page 129)

1. Bring a large pot of water to a boil. Add 2 tablespoons salt and the pasta and cook until just slightly under al dente, about 7 minutes. Reserve 1 cup of the pasta water and drain the pasta; set both aside.

2. While the pasta is cooking, heat the oil in a large high-sided sauté pan over medium heat until it begins to shimmer. Add the garlic and cook until soft, about 1 minute. Stir in the chile flakes and cook for 1 minute more. Stir in the anchovy and cook, stirring continuously, until it melts into the oil, about 1 minute more.

3. Increase the heat to high, add the wine, and cook until reduced by half. Add the butter, piece by piece, whisking until smooth. Add the pasta and toss with tongs to coat. Add the crab and some of the reserved pasta water to loosen up the sauce. Add the parsley, lemon zest, and salt and pepper to taste. Stir to combine.

4. Transfer to a shallow serving bowl and sprinkle the bread crumbs evenly over the top. Garnish with more lemon zest and parsley leaves, if desired, and serve.

(recipe continues)

Garlic Bread Crumbs

Makes 1 cup

2 tablespoons **olive oil**

2 tablespoons **unsalted butter**

2 **garlic cloves**, finely chopped to a paste with the side of a chef's knife and ¼ teaspoon kosher salt

1 cup **panko bread crumbs**

¼ teaspoon **kosher salt**

⅛ teaspoon **freshly ground black pepper**

1.   Heat the oil and butter in a large sauté pan over medium heat until the butter has melted and the mixture begins to shimmer. Add the garlic and cook, stirring continuously, until soft and lightly golden brown, about 2 minutes.

2.   Add the bread crumbs, salt, and pepper and cook, stirring occasionally, until golden brown and toasted, about 5 minutes. Transfer to a plate in an even layer to cool. Use immediately, or store in an airtight container in a cool, dark place for up to 2 days. To re-crisp, spread bread crumbs on a baking sheet and toast in a 300°F oven for 5 minutes.

Seafood Fra Diavalo Pasta with Scallion Vinaigrette

This dish has a special role at my home, starring as one of the Feast of the Seven Fishes on my Christmas Eve menu. I love the briny flavor of squid ink and the pop of color and bright acidity that the scallion vinaigrette adds to the dramatically dark dish. Lobster works well, too, and if squid ink isn't your thing, use regular pasta.

Serves 4 to 6

SCALLION VINAIGRETTE

¼ cup **white wine vinegar**

2 tablespoons chopped **shallot**

1 **garlic clove**, chopped

2 large **scallions**, green and pale green parts only, sliced

1 tablespoon **Dijon mustard**

1 teaspoon **clover honey**

¼ teaspoon **kosher salt**

¼ teaspoon **freshly ground black pepper**

½ cup **blended oil** (equal parts canola and extra-virgin olive oil)

PASTA

¼ cup **olive oil**

12 large **shrimp**, peeled and deveined

Kosher salt and **freshly ground black pepper**

12 ounces **squid**, thinly cut into rings and tentacles

5 **garlic cloves**, thinly sliced

¼ teaspoon **Calabrian chile flakes**

2 cups **Marinara Sauce** (page 126)

1 pound fresh **black squid ink pasta** (see variations, page 121)

¼ cup chopped fresh **flat-leaf parsley leaves**

¼ cup chopped fresh **basil leaves**

1. **Make the vinaigrette:** Combine the vinegar, shallot, garlic, scallions, mustard, honey, salt, and pepper in a blender and blend until smooth. With the motor running, slowly drizzle in the oil and blend until emulsified. The vinaigrette can be made up to 2 days in advance and stored, tightly covered, in the refrigerator.

2. **Make the pasta:** Heat the olive oil in a large high-sided sauté pan over medium-high heat until it begins to shimmer. Add the shrimp and season with salt and pepper. Cook until lightly golden on both sides, about 1 minute per side. Transfer to a plate. Add the squid to the pan and season with salt and pepper. Cook until lightly golden brown, about 1 minute. Transfer to the plate with the shrimp.

3. Add the garlic to the pan and cook until lightly golden brown, about 2 minutes. Add the chile flakes and cook for 20 seconds more. Add the marinara and bring to a boil. Reduce the heat to medium and simmer until the sauce has thickened, about 20 minutes.

4. While the sauce is cooking, bring a large pot of water to a boil. Add 2 tablespoons salt and the squid ink pasta and cook until it floats to the top of the pot and is al dente, about 3 to 4 minutes. (If using boxed dried pasta instead of fresh, cook it for 8 minutes.) Reserve 1 cup of the pasta cooking water and drain the pasta well. Set both aside.

5. Add the shrimp and squid to the tomato sauce. Bring the sauce to a simmer and cook until just heated through, about 2 minutes. Add the pasta and toss to coat with the sauce, adding some of the reserved pasta water, if needed. Add the parsley and basil and stir to combine.

6. Transfer to a large shallow bowl, drizzle the top with the vinaigrette, and serve.

MEAT

I meant every word I wrote in the intro the Vegetables & Sides chapter and yet, when it's time to call the troops to the table, you better believe that it's the Cast-Iron Porterhouse with Brown Butter and Blue Cheese (page 153) that gets them running. And man, there are some days when nothing else than the Perfect Burger (page 145), with its mouthwatering aroma second to perhaps only bacon, is going to satisfy—and satisfy it always does. This chapter isn't all indulgences, though there's plenty of room in the modern healthy diet for meat. Grilled Skirt Steak Caprese (page 157)—with its array of fresh tomatoes, summery basil, and just enough juicy, beefy skirt steak to make it meal-worthy—is a favorite light summer meal. Another fun Mediterranean twist is the Lamb Chop Milanese with Greek Salad Tzatziki (page 148); it seems like I'm on a mission to convert any and all guests at my table into lovers of Greek cuisine. Of course no cookbook would be complete without a perfect chicken recipe (and this one has a few), but I must say that my Brick Chicken with Salsa Verde (page 135) is not only one of my favorite recipes to make but a top requested dish that my guests ask for all year long.

Brick Chicken with Salsa Verde

In my opinion, the quintessential roasted chicken with salsa verde is served by my friend and mentor Jonathan Waxman at his restaurant Barbuto in New York City. Jonathan has been making that chicken at every restaurant he has owned for the past thirty years, and it is still as delicious as the first time he prepared it. This is my homage to that chicken dish, and one of my favorite things to prepare at home. Whether I am cooking the chicken on my grill in the summer or on the stovetop under a brick in the winter, it's always a hit with guests.

Serves 4

¾ cup **extra-virgin olive oil**

2 large **garlic cloves**, finely chopped

2 **anchovies packed in oil**, drained, patted dry, and finely chopped

Finely grated **zest of 1 lemon**

Pinch of **crushed red pepper flakes**

1 cup finely chopped fresh **flat-leaf parsley leaves**

¼ cup finely chopped fresh **tarragon leaves**

2 tablespoons finely sliced fresh **chives**

Kosher salt and **freshly ground black pepper**

1 (4-pound) **whole chicken**, cut into 8 pieces

Canola oil

1. Whisk together the olive oil, garlic, anchovies, lemon zest, and red pepper flakes in a small bowl. Stir in the parsley, tarragon, and chives and season with salt and black pepper. Let the salsa verde sit at room temperature while you cook the chicken to allow the flavors to meld.

2. Remove the chicken from the refrigerator 20 minutes before cooking. Season the chicken well on both sides with salt and black pepper.

3. Heat a 12-inch cast-iron skillet over medium-low heat. Coat the pan with a few teaspoons of canola oil. Wrap a brick in two layers of heavy-duty aluminum foil. (If you don't have a brick, use a heavy pan or bacon press.) Place the chicken in the pan, skin-side down, and place the foil-wrapped brick or pan on top of the chicken. Slowly cook over low heat until the fat renders and the skin begins to crisp and turn golden brown, about 10 minutes. Turn the chicken over and cook until it is just cooked through and registers 155°F on an instant-read thermometer, about 15 minutes more. Remove the chicken from the pan and let rest for 5 minutes. Serve drizzled with the salsa verde.

Chicken Parmesan

Chicken Parmesan I challenge you to find someone out there who won't succumb to a plate of chicken Parmesan. Put it on a sub or lay it on a dish of pasta; either way, the juicy chicken cutlets—encased in crispy, golden brown bread crumbs, smothered in bright marinara, and crowned with a bubbling layer of fresh mozzarella—will bring the hungry masses to their knees.

Serves 4

2 (12-ounce) boneless, skinless **chicken breasts**

2 cups **all-purpose flour**

4 large **eggs**, beaten

2 cups **bread crumbs**

Kosher salt and **freshly ground black pepper**

½ cup **canola oil**

1 pound **fresh mozzarella cheese**, thinly sliced

3 cups **Marinara Sauce** (page 126) or your favorite store-bought marinara sauce, warmed

Freshly grated **Parmigiano Reggiano cheese**

2 tablespoons fresh **lemon juice**

2 tablespoons **extra-virgin olive oil**

3 ounces **baby arugula**

1. Preheat the oven to 425°F. Working with one breast at a time, place chicken breasts on a cutting board, flat side down. Press the chicken with the palm of one hand, and cut in half horizontally to make 2 cutlets. With the flat side of a meat pounder, pound the chicken between pieces of plastic wrap until about ¼ inch thick.

2. Put the flour, beaten eggs, and bread crumbs in separate shallow dishes and season each with salt and pepper. Season each chicken cutlet on both sides with salt and pepper. Dredge each cutlet in the flour and tap off any excess. Dip in the eggs and let the excess drip off. Dredge in the bread crumbs, pressing the crumbs to adhere to the chicken. Transfer the breaded chicken to a baking sheet or large plate.

3. Place a wire rack over a rimmed baking sheet. Heat ¼ cup of the canola oil in a large sauté pan over high heat until it begins to shimmer. Add 2 pieces of the chicken to the hot oil and cook until golden brown on both sides, about 3 minutes per side. Transfer the chicken to the wire rack on the baking sheet. Heat the remaining ¼ cup canola oil and cook the remaining chicken.

4. Divide the mozzarella evenly among the chicken breasts. Place the baking sheet in the oven and bake until the cheese is melted and golden brown, about 5 minutes.

5. Remove the chicken from the oven. Put one chicken breast on each of four plates, ladle hot marinara sauce over the top, and sprinkle with grated Parmigiano Reggiano.

6. In a large bowl, whisk together the lemon juice and olive oil. Add the arugula and season with salt and pepper. Top each plate with some arugula and serve.

Korean BBQ Chicken If you get invited to a pool party at my home in the summer, there is a good chance you will be eating a platter of this all day long. I am obsessed with the fermented Korean chile paste gochujang and love using it in marinades, glazes, and vinaigrettes. Orange juice and honey add sweetness and help create an incredible texture. I love serving this with Napa Slaw with Kimchi Vinaigrette (page 90), grilled corn slathered with scallion butter, and lots of ice-cold beer. Summertime at its best!

Serves 4 to 6

2 (4-pound) **whole chickens**, cut into
    8 pieces each, patted dry

1 cup **gochujang**

½ cup fresh **orange juice**

¼ cup **clover honey**

¼ cup **light soy sauce**

2 tablespoons **toasted sesame oil**

Canola oil

Kosher salt and **freshly ground
    black pepper**

2 **green scallions**, green and pale
    green parts only, thinly sliced

NOTE Cooking over charcoal gives this chicken another layer of flavor, but if you only have a gas grill or a grill pan, it will be tasty, too.

1. Put the chicken pieces in a large bowl and, using a paring knife, make a few slashes in the skin of each piece.

2. Whisk together the gochujang, orange juice, honey, soy sauce, and sesame oil in a medium bowl. Add half the marinade to the bowl with the chicken and mix the chicken well to make sure each piece is coated. Cover and refrigerate the chicken for at least 2 hours and up to 8 hours. Set the remaining marinade aside for grilling.

3. Line a baking sheet with paper towels. Remove the chicken from the refrigerator 30 minutes before cooking and set it on the paper towel–lined baking sheet; pat dry.

4. Prepare a charcoal (or gas) grill for indirect-heat grilling or heat a grill pan over medium heat.

5. Brush the chicken pieces with canola oil on both sides and season lightly with salt and pepper (remember that the marinade contains soy sauce, which is salty).

6. *If using an outdoor grill:* Place the chicken pieces skin-side down on the grill grates over indirect heat; close the lid. Cook for about 15 minutes, until the fat begins to render and the skin gets golden brown and crispy. Brush the top with some of the reserved marinade, turn the chicken over, cover the grill, and cook for 10 minutes more. Brush with the marinade and turn the pieces again. Move the chicken over direct heat and cook, turning once again, until the skin is well browned and crisp, 3 to 5 minutes.

(recipe continues)

If using a grill pan: Put the chicken on the grill pan, skin-side down, and cook until the fat renders and the skin begins to form a crust and turn golden brown, about 8 minutes (the chicken is ready to turn when the skin releases easily from the pan). Flip the chicken pieces and cook until golden brown on the second side. Brush the top with some of the reserved marinade. Turn the chicken again, cover the pan, and cook for 5 minutes more. Brush with the marinade, turn the pieces again, and cook for 5 minutes more.

7. Brush the chicken with marinade a final time and transfer to a platter. Let rest, loosely tented with foil, for 7 minutes before serving. (The chicken should register 155°F on an instant-read thermometer when removed from the grill. The carryover cooking during the resting period will increase the heat to about 162°F, which is perfect.) Serve on a platter and garnish with green onions.

Fried Chicken Tenders with Horseradish–Honey Mustard Sauce

"Chicken nuggets for adults" is how I refer to these golden strips of perfection. Marinating in yogurt and using dark meat chicken ensures tender, flavorful meat every time. Using boneless thighs just makes it easier to eat and faster to cook, while adding cornstarch to the flour dredge creates extra crispiness.

Serves 4

HORSERADISH–HONEY MUSTARD SAUCE

¾ cup **Dijon mustard**

¾ cup **whole-grain mustard**

¼ cup prepared **horseradish**, drained

¼ cup **clover honey**

½ teaspoon **kosher salt**

⅛ teaspoon **freshly ground black pepper**

CHICKEN

2 cups **nonfat Greek yogurt**

¾ cup **whole milk**

1 teaspoon **ground chiles de árbol**

Kosher salt and **freshly ground black pepper**

8 boneless, skinless **chicken thighs**, each sliced lengthwise into 3 equal pieces

1¾ cups **all-purpose flour**

¼ cup **cornstarch**

1 teaspoon **garlic powder**

1 teaspoon **onion powder**

Canola oil

1. **Make the horseradish–honey mustard sauce:** Whisk together the mustards, horseradish, honey, salt, and pepper in a small bowl. Cover and refrigerate for at least 1 hour and up to 24 hours to allow the flavors to meld. Remove from the refrigerator 30 minutes before serving.

2. **Marinate the chicken:** In a large bowl, whisk together 1 cup yogurt, ¼ cup of the milk, the chile de árbol, 2 teaspoons salt, and ½ teaspoon pepper until combined. Add the chicken and toss to coat evenly with the marinade. Cover and refrigerate for at least 4 hours and up to 24 hours.

3. Remove the chicken from the refrigerator and rinse under cold water to remove the marinade. Pat dry with paper towels and season with salt and pepper.

4. In a medium bowl, whisk together the remaining 1 cup yogurt and ½ cup milk and season with 1 teaspoon salt and a pinch of pepper. Whisk together the flour, cornstarch, garlic powder, onion powder, 1 tablespoon salt, and ½ teaspoon pepper in a large baking dish until combined. Working in batches, dip the chicken pieces in the yogurt mixture, letting any excess drip off, then dredge them in the flour mixture, tapping off any excess.

5. Set a wire rack over a rimmed baking sheet and keep it nearby. Fill a large cast-iron pan with oil to a depth of 2 inches. Heat the oil over medium heat until it begins to shimmer. Working in batches, add the chicken to the hot oil and fry until golden brown on both sides and just cooked through, about 3 minutes per side. Transfer to the wire rack over the baking sheet. Repeat to fry the remaining chicken.

6. Serve the chicken with the horseradish–honey mustard sauce on the side.

Turkey Posole with Crispy Hominy

This is a great soup to make with leftover turkey the day after Thanksgiving, but you can substitute rotisserie chicken and eat it any time you want. If you aren't big on chard, any green will do, and as always, including greens adds lots of extra nutrients. So easy, flavorful, and satisfying, it's everything a soup should be.

Serves 4 to 6

6 cups **Chicken Stock** (page 237) or low-sodium store-bought chicken stock or broth

2 **ancho chiles**, soaked in water to soften, then drained

1 ounce **dried porcini mushrooms**, soaked in water until soft, drained, and chopped

3 cups shredded **roasted turkey** or rotisserie chicken meat

1 small bunch **chard** or kale, stems removed, leaves cut into thin ribbons (about 4 cups)

3 tablespoons chopped fresh **cilantro leaves**, plus whole leaves for garnish

Kosher salt and **freshly ground black pepper**

Juice of 2 limes (about ¼ cup)

3 tablespoons **canola oil**

1 (28-ounce) can **hominy**, drained, rinsed, and patted dry with paper towels

Lime wedges, for garnish

1. Place 5¾ cups of the stock in a medium saucepan and bring to a simmer over medium-low heat. Place the remaining ¼ cup stock and the rehydrated ancho chiles in a blender and purée until combined.

2. Add the puréed anchos and porcinis to the saucepan with the stock and return the mixture to a simmer. Add the turkey, chard, and cilantro and cook until the chard is wilted and the turkey is heated through, about 5 minutes. Season with salt and pepper and add the lime juice.

3. While the soup is cooking, heat the oil in a large nonstick pan over high heat until it begins to shimmer. Line a plate with paper towels and set it nearby. Add the hominy to the hot oil and cook, stirring occasionally, until lightly golden brown and crispy, about 5 minutes. Transfer to the paper towel–lined plate and immediately sprinkle with a bit of salt.

4. Ladle the soup into bowls. Top with some of the crispy hominy, cilantro, and a lime wedge alongside and serve.

The Perfect Burger Yes, I have written a book called *Burgers, Fries & Shakes*. Yes, I have many Bobby's Burger Palace locations. Yes, I have made this burger a hundred times on TV. Having said all that, one of the top five cooking questions that I continue to get is, "Hey, Bobby, how do I make a perfect burger?" So here we go again. Five important parts: First, the meat needs to be top-quality Grade A chuck with 80 percent lean and 20 percent fat. Second, you need to season the burger heavily (on the outside only) with salt and pepper. You need to cook it in a cast-iron pan. If using cheese, you need to let the cheese melt completely. Finally, the bun (with sesame seeds, whenever possible) needs to be soft and lightly toasted. There you go.

Serves 4

1½ pounds **80% lean ground chuck**

Kosher salt and **freshly ground black pepper**

1 tablespoon **canola oil**

8 thin slices **white American cheese**

4 soft **hamburger buns** with sesame seeds (such as Martin's), halved and lightly toasted

1. Divide the meat into four equal 6-ounce portions. Loosely form each portion into a ¾-inch-thick patty. Generously season both sides with salt and pepper. Make a deep depression in the center of each with your thumb.

2. Heat the oil in a large cast-iron pan over high heat until it begins to shimmer. Put the patties in the pan and cook until golden brown on the bottom, about 4 minutes. Flip the patties and cook until golden brown on the second side and cooked to your desired doneness, about 4 minutes more for medium (my preference).

3. Make sure you have the pan lid on hand. Add 2 slices of the cheese to each burger. Add ¼ cup warm water to the pan (be careful—it will splatter and make a lot of noise) and immediately cover the pan and count to 20. Do not lift the lid. After 20 seconds, lift the lid to make sure that the cheese is completely melted. If it isn't, cover the pan and cook for 10 seconds more.

4. Place a patty on each of the buns and top with your favorite toppings.

Green Chile Cheeseburger

Green Chile Cheeseburger It is no secret that I love all things chile and Southwest, and this burger is no exception. If you ever get the chance to go to Santa Fe, New Mexico, one of the first things you should eat is one of these. In New Mexico, they use the delicious Hatch green chile, grown in the Hatch Valley. The chile's season is very short, about six weeks between August and September, so they are nearly impossible to get fresh in most of the country. Occasionally, you can find them frozen online. If I can't get them, I just use all poblano or substitute a few Cubanelle chiles in their place. As a lifelong New Yorker, of course my version is a bit fancier, with the addition of queso sauce, pickled red onions, and blue corn tortillas for some added crunch.

Serves 4

GREEN CHILE RELISH

1 medium **poblano chile**, roasted, peeled, seeded, and thinly sliced (see Tip; page 54)

2 **Hatch chiles**, roasted, peeled, seeded, and thinly sliced (see Tip; page 54)

1 **serrano chile**, roasted, peeled, seeded, and thinly sliced (see Tip; page 54)

¼ cup **red wine vinegar**

1 tablespoon **clover honey**

2 tablespoons **extra-virgin olive oil**

3 tablespoons chopped fresh **cilantro**

Kosher salt and **freshly ground black pepper**

1. **Make the relish:** Combine the roasted chiles, vinegar, honey, oil, and cilantro in a medium bowl and season with salt and pepper. Let sit at room temperature for at least 30 minutes before serving. The relish can be made 1 day in advance and stored, covered, in the refrigerator; bring to room temperature before serving.

2. **Make the queso sauce:** Melt the butter in a small saucepan over medium heat. Whisk in the flour and cook for 1 minute. Add the milk, increase the heat to high, and cook, whisking continuously, until slightly thickened, about 5 minutes. Remove from the heat and whisk in the Chihuahua cheese until melted; add the Parmigiano Reggiano and season with salt and pepper. Keep warm until ready to serve.

3. Put a burger on the bottom bun and spoon several tablespoons of the queso sauce on top of the burger. Top the queso with a few large spoonfuls of the green chile relish, blue corn chips, and some pickled red onions. Repeat with the remaining burgers and serve.

1 tablespoon **unsalted butter**

1 tablespoon **all-purpose flour**

1 cup **whole milk**

8 ounces **Chihuahua** or **Monterey Jack cheese**, coarsely grated

¼ cup grated **Parmigiano Reggiano cheese**

Kosher salt and **freshly ground black pepper**

4 **Perfect Burgers** (page 145), without the cheese

12 **blue corn tortilla chips**, coarsely crushed

¼ cup **Pickled Red Onions** (page 248)

Lamb Chop Milanese with Greek Salad Tzatziki

I love Greek food—it's always fresh, full of flavor, and really healthy, even when you are frying a portion of it. Of course, you can just grill or pan-roast the lamb for a healthier version, but I say prepare it this way and just run an extra mile the next morning.

Serves 4

LAMB

1¼ pounds **Frenched lamb chops** (trimmed of excess fat)

¼ cup **olive oil**

7 **garlic cloves**, smashed to a paste with the side of a chef's knife and ¼ teaspoon kosher salt

¼ cup finely chopped fresh **oregano**

Finely grated **zest of 1 lemon**

2 cups **all-purpose flour**

3 large **eggs**, beaten

2 cups **panko bread crumbs**

Kosher salt and **freshly ground black pepper**

½ cup **blended oil** (equal parts canola and extra-virgin olive oil)

GREEK SALAD TZATZIKI

1 cup halved **grape tomatoes**

¼ teaspoon **kosher salt**, plus more as needed

¼ teaspoon **freshly ground black pepper**, plus more as needed

1 tablespoon **red wine vinegar**

Finely grated **zest of 1 lemon**

1 teaspoon **Dijon mustard**

¼ teaspoon dried **oregano**

1. Marinate the lamb: Put the lamb chops in a large baking dish. Whisk together the olive oil, garlic, oregano, and lemon zest in a small bowl. Pour the marinade over the lamb and turn to coat. Cover and refrigerate for at least 1 hour and up to 8 hours.

2. Make the salad: Mix together the tomatoes, salt, pepper, vinegar, lemon zest, mustard, oregano, and garlic in a small bowl and let sit at room temperature for at least 15 minutes and up to 2 hours to allow the flavors to meld.

3. Put the yogurt in a large bowl. Using a slotted spoon, add the tomato mixture to the yogurt (leaving as much of the liquid behind as possible). Add the olives, onion, feta, and parsley and gently fold to combine. Season with salt and pepper. Cover and refrigerate for at least 30 minutes and up to 4 hours.

4. Remove the lamb from the refrigerator 30 minutes before cooking. Pat the chops dry with paper towels. On a cutting board, lay out one lamb chop and place a piece of plastic wrap on top. Using a meat mallet, pound the chop to ¼-inch thickness. Repeat with the remaining chops.

5. Put the flour, eggs, and panko in separate shallow bowls or baking dishes. Season each with salt and pepper. Dredge the lamb chops in the flour, shaking off any excess. Dip in the eggs, letting any excess drip off, then dredge in the panko to coat.

2 large **garlic cloves**, smashed and chopped to a paste with the side of a chef's knife and ¼ teaspoon kosher salt

2 cups **2% Greek yogurt**

½ cup finely diced **pitted kalamata olives**

¼ cup finely diced **red onion**

¼ cup crumbled **Greek feta cheese**

¼ cup chopped fresh **flat-leaf parsley leaves**

6. Heat ¼ cup of the oil in a large skillet over medium-high heat until it begins to shimmer. Line a plate with paper towels and set it nearby. Add 2 of the lamb chops to the hot oil and cook until golden, about 3 minutes. Flip and cook until golden on the second side, 2 to 3 minutes more. Transfer to the paper towel–lined plate. Heat the remaining ¼ cup oil in the pan and cook the remaining lamb chops.

7. Top the lamb with the Greek salad tzatziki just before serving.

Pressure-Cooked Ropa Vieja

Ropa vieja (Spanish for "old clothes") is the national dish of Cuba and comfort food at its best. Typically made with flank steak and braised in the oven for several hours, I prefer using the fattier, more flavorful chuck roast for my version, and being an impatient New Yorker, I use a pressure cooker to decrease the cooking time by about 1½ hours. Any leftovers are perfect for sandwiches (see page 161).

Serves 4, with leftovers for sandwiches

Kosher salt and **freshly ground black pepper**

2 teaspoons **ground cumin**

2 teaspoons **ground coriander**

4 pounds **chuck roast**, brisket, or flank steak, trimmed of excess fat and cut into 2-inch pieces for the chuck and brisket or into 3 equal pieces for the flank

3 tablespoons **canola oil**

1 large **Spanish onion**, halved and thinly sliced

1 **yellow bell pepper**, thinly sliced

1 **poblano chile**, seeded and diced

5 **garlic cloves**, smashed

1 cup **dry sherry**

3 cups homemade **Chicken Stock** (page 237), or store-bought low-sodium chicken or beef canned stock or broth

⅓ cup **golden raisins**

½ cup **Spanish green olives**, pitted and thinly sliced

2 tablespoons **capers**, drained

¼ cup fresh **lime juice**

3 tablespoons chopped fresh **cilantro leaves**

Crispy Coconut-Scallion Rice (page 105) or flour tortillas, for serving

1. Combine 1 tablespoon salt, 1 teaspoon black pepper, the cumin, and coriander in a small bowl. Season the meat on both sides with the spice rub, making sure to rub the spices in completely.

2. Heat 2 tablespoons of the oil in a large high-sided sauté pan over high heat until it begins to shimmer. Working in batches, add the meat to the hot oil and sear until golden brown on all sides, about 8 minutes. Remove using a slotted spoon and transfer the meat to a pressure cooker.

3. Add the remaining 1 tablespoon oil to the pan, if needed, and add the onion, bell pepper, and poblano. Cook, stirring occasionally, until soft, about 4 minutes. Add the garlic and cook for 1 minute more. Add the sherry and cook until reduced by half, about 5 minutes. Add 2 cups of the stock and bring to a boil.

4. Carefully pour the hot mixture over the beef in the pressure cooker and sprinkle the raisins around the pot. Put the lid on and follow the manufacturer's directions to bring it to pressure. Cook the roast until fork-tender, about 40 minutes. Transfer the beef to a cutting board, loosely tent with foil, and let rest for 15 minutes.

5. Transfer the contents of the pressure cooker to a large saucepan and add the remaining 1 cup stock, the olives, and capers. Bring to a boil and cook until slightly reduced. Remove from the heat and add the lime juice and chopped cilantro.

6. Carefully shred the meat by pulling it apart into long fibers with two forks. Add the meat to the sauce and stir to heat through. Serve with coconut-scallion rice or flour tortillas.

TIP If your pressure cooker has a sauté function, you can do everything in one pot. If you don't have a pressure cooker at all and, unlike me, are patient, you can make this in a large pot with a lid and braise it in a preheated 325°F oven for about 2 hours instead.

Cast-Iron Porterhouse with Brown Butter and Blue Cheese

I stole this preparation from *the* steakhouse of all steakhouses, Peter Luger in Brooklyn, New York. Yes, it may seem strange to cook a steak halfway in a pan on top of the stove, slice it, then finish cooking it under the broiler—but it works! Trust me. If you have never cooked your steak this way, be prepared to eat the best steak of your life, even if you can't get to Brooklyn.

Serves 4

1 (2-inch thick) bone-in **porterhouse steak** (about 2 pounds), trimmed

Kosher salt and **freshly ground black pepper**

2 tablespoons **canola oil**

½ cup (1 stick) **unsalted butter**, cut into pieces, at room temperature

8 ounces **Maytag blue cheese**, crumbled

1 teaspoon chopped fresh **thyme leaves**

1. Remove the steak from the refrigerator 30 minutes before cooking. Preheat the broiler.

2. Season the steak very generously on all sides with salt and pepper.

3. Heat the oil in a large (preferably cast-iron) skillet over medium-high heat until it begins to shimmer. Add the steak and cook until a deep brown crust forms on the bottom, about 4 minutes. Remove the skillet from the heat and transfer the steak to a cutting board, browned-side up.

4. Using a sharp knife, cut the meat off the bone in two whole pieces (rib eye and fillet). Slice both pieces 1 inch thick across the grain. Reassemble the sliced steak around the bone (it should look like a whole sliced steak) and return it to the skillet, browned-side up.

5. Top with the butter and lightly season with salt. Broil, stopping and spooning some of the butter on top, until the steak is cooked to medium-rare (you can peek between slices to check the doneness), 4 to 6 minutes, depending on the thickness of the steak. During the last 45 seconds, sprinkle the cheese over the top. Remove the pan from the oven, add the thyme to the melted butter in the pan, and spoon the buttery sauce over the steak. Serve immediately.

Green Pork Chili

When I decided to include this recipe in the book, I asked myself, *Why don't I make this chili more often?* It is delicious, simple, and perfect for when the weather turns cooler and Sunday afternoons are spent in front of the TV watching football with your good friends. Any kind of braised dish is best made the day before and refrigerated overnight before serving. So, if you can, make it on a Saturday and serve it on Sunday.

Serves 4 to 6

1 large **red onion**, chopped

1 pound **tomatillos**, husked, scrubbed, and halved

3 **jalapeños**, halved and seeded

5 **garlic cloves**, smashed

5 tablespoons **canola oil**

Kosher salt and **freshly ground black pepper**

½ cup chopped fresh **cilantro leaves**, plus more for garnish

Juice of 1 lime

3 pounds **boneless pork shoulder**, cut into 1-inch cubes

4 cups **Chicken Stock** (page 237)

Crème fraîche (optional)

Pickled Red Onions (page 248)

Lime wedges

1. Preheat the oven to 400°F.

2. In a large bowl, toss the onion, tomatillos, jalapeños, and garlic with 2 tablespoons of the oil and spread on a baking sheet. Season with salt and pepper. Roast until soft and lightly charred, 25 to 30 minutes, stirring twice during roasting. Transfer the vegetables to a food processor. Add the cilantro and lime juice and purée until smooth.

3. Reduce the oven temperature to 325°F.

4. While the vegetables are in the oven, heat the remaining 3 tablespoons oil in a large Dutch oven over high heat until it begins to shimmer. Working in batches, add the pork and cook until well browned. Remove with a slotted spoon and transfer to a bowl. Drain the oil from the pot and return the pork to the pot.

5. Add the stock and the tomatillo purée to the pork and stir to combine. Cover the pot, transfer to the oven, and cook until the pork is fork-tender, about 1½ hours.

6. Ladle into bowls and serve topped with crème fraîche (if using), cilantro, pickled onions, and the lime wedges.

Grilled Skirt Steak Caprese

I make this on those really hot summer days when you want something light and delicious and tomatoes are at their best. Skirt steak takes only a few minutes to cook, and while it's resting, you can put together the salad. If skirt steak isn't available, flank or strip work really well, too. Adding thinly sliced mozzarella will make it a true caprese.

Serves 4 to 6

VINAIGRETTE

½ cup **balsamic vinegar**

2 teaspoons **Dijon mustard**

¼ teaspoon **kosher salt**

¼ teaspoon **freshly ground black pepper**

½ cup **canola oil**

2 pounds **skirt steak**, halved lengthwise

Kosher salt and **freshly ground black pepper**

4 ounces **baby arugula**

1 small **red onion**, halved and thinly sliced

4 ripe **beefsteak tomatoes**, thinly sliced

1. **Make the vinaigrette:** Whisk together the vinegar, mustard, salt, and pepper in a medium bowl. While whisking, slowly drizzle in the oil and whisk until emulsified. Set aside.

2. Place the steak in a baking dish. Add half the vinaigrette and turn to coat; let the steak sit at room temperature for 30 minutes.

3. Heat a grill to high or a grill pan over high heat on top of the stove.

4. Remove the steak from the marinade and pat dry. Season both sides with salt and pepper. Grill until lightly charred on both sides and just cooked to medium-rare doneness, about 4 minutes per side. Transfer the steak to a cutting board and let rest for 5 minutes.

5. Meanwhile, mix together the arugula and red onion in a large bowl. Add some of the remaining vinaigrette and toss to coat. Season with salt and pepper.

6. Thinly slice the steak across the grain and arrange it on a platter with the tomatoes. Serve with the arugula salad.

Grilled Pork Chops with Peppers and Balsamic

Growing up in New York City, the majority of my friends were Italian, and any chance that I got, I was eating dinner at their houses. This dish reminds me of those dinners and screams "American Southern Italian" to me. I prepare it often in the summer, and each time I eat it, I am transported back to my childhood. My modern spin is the balsamic reduction, which I am almost certain did not exist in New York City in the early 1970s. The relish and glaze work really nicely with grilled chicken and steak-like fishes such as tuna and swordfish, too.

Serves 4

BALSAMIC SAUCE

2 cups good-quality **balsamic vinegar** (not expensive, just good quality)

2 teaspoons **clover honey**

GLAZE

½ cup good-quality **balsamic vinegar**

¼ cup **clover honey**

¼ cup **canola oil**

2 tablespoons chopped fresh **flat-leaf parsley leaves**

1 tablespoon finely chopped fresh **thyme**

PORK

4 **bone-in center-cut pork chops**, each about 12 ounces and 1 inch thick

Canola oil

Kosher salt and **freshly ground black pepper**

Hot and Sweet Pepper Relish (page 160)

Fresh **flat-leaf parsley leaves**, for garnish

1. **Make the balsamic sauce:** Put the vinegar in a nonreactive pan (such as stainless steel). Bring to a boil over high heat and cook until reduced to ½ cup, about 20 minutes. Stir in the honey, transfer to a bowl, and let cool to room temperature; it will thicken as it cools.

2. **Make the glaze:** Whisk together the vinegar, honey, oil, parsley, and thyme in a medium bowl and let sit at room temperature for 30 minutes.

3. **Cook the pork:** Remove the pork from the refrigerator 30 minutes before grilling to take the chill off.

4. Heat a grill to high or a cast-iron grill pan over high heat.

5. Brush the pork chops on both sides with canola oil and season with salt and pepper. Grill on one side until golden brown, about 4 minutes. Flip the pork chops and grill on the second side until golden brown, about 4 minutes longer. Brush with some of the glaze, flip, brush with more glaze, and flip again. Cook until a crust forms on the pork and the meat is cooked through (it should register 145°F on an instant-read thermometer), 10 to 12 minutes total.

6. Transfer the chops to a plate, top with some of the relish, and drizzle with the balsamic sauce. Garnish with parsley leaves and serve.

(recipe continues)

Hot and Sweet Pepper Relish

Makes about 2 cups

2 **red bell peppers**

2 **yellow bell peppers**

2 tablespoons **canola oil**

Kosher salt and **freshly ground black pepper**

¼ cup **balsamic vinegar**

4 **garlic cloves**, mashed into a paste with the side of a chef's knife and ¼ teaspoon kosher salt

1 tablespoon **clover honey**

½ cup chopped fresh **flat-leaf parsley leaves**

½ cup chopped **seeded hot cherry peppers**

1. Preheat the oven to 425°F.

2. Put the bell peppers on a baking sheet, toss with oil, and season with salt and black pepper. Roast, turning once, until charred on both sides, about 25 minutes total. Transfer the peppers to a bowl, tightly cover with plastic wrap, and let steam for 10 minutes. Peel and seed the peppers; discard the skin and seeds and chop the flesh.

3. Whisk together the vinegar, garlic, honey, and parsley in a large bowl and season with salt and black pepper. Add the roasted bell peppers and the cherry peppers and toss to coat. Let sit at room temperature for at least 30 minutes before serving to allow the flavors to meld. The relish can be made up to 8 hours in advance and stored, covered, in the refrigerator; bring to room temperature before serving.

Cuban Beef Sandwiches
This is a great way to use leftover Ropa Vieja from the night before—think of it as Cuba meets Spain meets Chicago meets delicious.

Serves 2

¼ cup **mayonnaise**, such as Hellmann's

1 heaping tablespoon **Dijon mustard**

¼ cup **cooking liquid from Pressure-Cooked Ropa Vieja** (page 150), including some of the capers, olives, and herbs

2 long soft **hoagie rolls**, split

¼ pound **Manchego cheese**, coarsely grated or thinly sliced

2 cups **Pressure-Cooked Ropa Vieja** (page 150), heated

⅓ cup **Pickled Red Onions** (page 248)

2 tablespoons **unsalted butter**, softened

Plantain chips, for serving

1. Combine the mayonnaise, mustard, and cooking liquid in a small food processor and process until smooth. Scrape into a bowl, cover, and refrigerate for at least 30 minutes and up to 1 day.

2. Spread the mayonnaise mixture over the cut sides of each roll. Add 2 slices of the cheese to each. Divide the beef evenly between the rolls and top with the pickled onions. Close the rolls.

3. Heat a cast-iron pan over low heat until hot to the touch or heat a panini press according to the manufacturer's instructions. Wrap a brick in two layers of heavy-duty aluminum foil. (If you don't have a brick, use a heavy pan or bacon press.) Brush the top of each roll with 1 tablespoon of the butter and place the sandwiches in the pan, buttered-side down, and set the foil-wrapped brick or pan on top of them (or put them in the panini press and cook according to the manufacturer's directions). Cook, turning the sandwiches halfway through, until the bread is golden brown on both sides and the cheese has melted, about 6 minutes.

4. Serve the sandwiches with the plantain chips.

SEAFOOD

I have heard from more than one person that while they love seafood and almost always order it when dining out, they never make it at home. That is most definitely not me. I say, make friends with your fishmonger (whether a pro at a fancy fish market or the guy behind the counter at your grocery store) and learn to trust your eyes and nose when making your selection. Be flexible with your recipe planning: Say you were craving Grilled Grouper with Balsam Farms Tomatoes and Avocado (page 179), but the grouper offered was less than stellar. Make a swap for a firm, white-fleshed fish that does look good. If you're worried about your kitchen smelling, it won't—but if it does, just light a candle. Life is too short to miss out on the joys of slurping great vats of brothy Moules Marinières (page 174) at your own table.

Baked Clams Barcelona

Baked Clams Barcelona I cook seafood often at home, too, and I love serving this as a precursor to a Spanish-inspired dinner at my New York apartment, or as one of the seven dishes I make for the Feast of the Seven Fishes at Christmastime.

Serves 4

CLAMS

1 cup **dry white wine**

1 large **shallot**, chopped

5 **garlic cloves**, chopped

2 sprigs **thyme**

24 **littleneck clams**, scrubbed

FILLING

2 tablespoons **canola oil**

4 ounces **Spanish chorizo**, removed from its casing, finely diced

1 large **shallot**, finely diced

2 **garlic cloves**, finely chopped to a paste with the side of a chef's knife and ¼ teapoon kosher salt

1 teaspoon **smoked Spanish paprika**

2 teaspoons finely chopped fresh **oregano**

½ cup **panko bread crumbs**

Kosher salt and **freshly ground black pepper**

¼ cup **mayonnaise**

½ teaspoon finely grated **lemon zest**

2 tablespoons finely chopped fresh **flat-leaf parsley leaves**

2 tablespoons **extra-virgin olive oil**

1. Cook the clams: Combine the wine, shallot, garlic, and thyme in a large Dutch oven and bring to a boil over high heat. Add the clams, stir a few times, and cover. Cook, shaking the pot a few times, until all the clams open, about 3 minutes.

2. Remove the clams using a slotted spoon and transfer to a large bowl, discarding any clams that have not opened. Strain the cooking liquid through a fine-mesh strainer into a medium bowl and set aside.

3. Let the clams cool slightly, then coarsely chop the meat and transfer to a small bowl, reserving the shells. Break 12 of the shells at the joint so you have 24 half shells and arrange them on a rimmed baking sheet; discard the remaining shells.

4. Make the filling: Preheat the boiler and line a plate with paper towels. Heat the canola oil in a medium sauté pan over high heat until it begins to shimmer. Add the chorizo and cook, breaking it up into small pieces, until golden brown, about 5 minutes. Remove with a slotted spoon and transfer to the paper towel–lined plate.

5. Remove all but 2 tablespoons of the fat from the pan. Add the shallot and cook over medium heat until soft, about 4 minutes. Add the garlic and cook for 30 seconds. Return the chorizo to the pan and add ½ cup of the reserved clam liquid, the paprika, and oregano. Bring to a boil and cook until the liquid has completely reduced, about 5 minutes. Stir in the chopped clams and cook for 30 seconds. Add ¼ cup of the panko and cook until combined. Season with salt and pepper. Transfer to a medium bowl and stir in the mayonnaise and zest.

6. Combine the remaining ¼ cup panko and the parsley in a small bowl. Add the olive oil and mix to combine. Fill each shell with the clam filling and sprinkle with the panko topping. Pour 1 cup water into the baking sheet. Broil, watching carefully, until golden brown and bubbling, 1 to 3 minutes. Serve immediately.

Oven-Roasted Shrimp Diavolo

The American Southwest meets Italy meets Spain in my version of *gambas al ajillo* (garlic shrimp). I love making and serving this in a *cazuela*, but you can use a regular baking dish. Serve with lots of crusty bread or over pasta or rice.

Serves 4

GARLIC CHIPS

½ cup **canola oil**

5 **garlic cloves**, thinly sliced

Kosher salt

24 extra-jumbo **shrimp** (16 to 20 count), peeled and deveined

1 cup **Chile Oil** (recipe follows)

1 tablespoon chopped fresh **oregano leaves**

Kosher salt and **freshly ground black pepper**

2 tablespoons finely chopped fresh **chives**

French bread, toasted and torn into pieces (optional), for dipping

1. **Make the garlic chips:** Line a plate with paper towels and set it nearby. Heat the oil in a small saucepan over medium heat until it begins to shimmer. Add the garlic, in batches, and fry until lightly golden brown, stirring to keep the slices from sticking to each other, about 2 minutes. Remove with a slotted spoon and transfer to the paper towel–lined plate. Season with a touch of salt. Repeat with the remaining garlic and set aside. If not using the garlic chips immediately, let cool completely and store in an airtight container in a cool, dark place for up to 2 days.

2. Preheat the oven to 425°F.

3. Combine the shrimp, ¾ cup of the chile oil and the oregano in a large *cazuela* or baking dish. Season with salt and pepper and roast until golden brown and just cooked through, turning once, about 8 minutes. Remove from the oven.

4. Drizzle with the remaining ¼ cup chile oil and garnish with the chives and garlic chips. Serve with the bread.

Chile Oil

Makes about 1¼ cups

2 **New Mexico chiles**, stemmed

2 **chiles de árbol**, stemmed

¼ teaspoon **Calabrian chile flakes**

1 cup **blended oil** (equal parts canola and extra-virgin olive oil)

4 **garlic cloves**, chopped

2 tablespoons fresh **thyme leaves**

2 teaspoons chopped fresh **oregano leaves**

½ teaspoon **kosher salt**

1. Heat a medium pan over medium heat. Add the New Mexico and árbol chiles and toast on both sides until fragrant and the color has deepened, about 5 minutes.

2. Combine the chiles, chile flakes, oil, garlic, thyme, oregano, and salt in a blender and blend until smooth, about 2 minutes. Transfer to a bowl, cover tightly, and refrigerate for at least 12 hours and up to 24 hours. Remove from the refrigerator 30 minutes before using. The chile oil will keep in the refrigerator, tightly covered, for up to 3 days.

Coconut–Red Curry Spot Prawns

Southeast Asian food is nothing like the Mediterranean or American cuisine that I cook and am known for, but I love curry, and the more I make it, the better it gets. I love that this is a one-pot meal, because as anyone who has ever been invited to dinner at my house knows, I love cooking but hate the cleanup. You can serve this with Crispy Coconut-Scallion Rice (page 105) or just plain rice or noodles. And FYI, this sauce is also great with chicken and pork.

Serves 4 to 6

4 tablespoons **canola oil**

24 extra-large **spot prawns** (16 to 20 count), peeled and deveined

Kosher salt and **freshly ground black pepper**

2 **shallots**, thinly sliced

1 medium **Spanish onion**, finely diced

5 **garlic cloves**, finely chopped to a paste with the side of a chef's knife and ¼ teaspoon kosher salt

1 (4-ounce) can **Maesri red curry paste**

1 (14-ounce) can **unsweetened coconut milk**

1 cup **Shrimp Stock** (page 239), Fish Stock (page 237), or water

1 tablespoon **fish sauce**

Grated **zest and juice of 2 limes**

¼ cup chopped fresh **cilantro leaves**

¼ cup fresh **Thai basil leaves**, torn (if you can't find it, use Italian basil)

1. Heat 3 tablespoons of the oil in a Dutch oven over high heat until it begins to shimmer. Season the prawns on both sides with salt and pepper. Working in batches if needed, add the shrimp to the pan in an even layer and sear until just golden brown on both sides but not cooked through, about 1 minute per side. Transfer the shrimp to a plate.

2. Add the remaining 1 tablespoon oil to the pan and heat until it begins to shimmer. Add the shallots and onion and cook until soft, about 4 minutes. Add the garlic and cook for 1 minute more.

3. Add the curry paste and cook, stirring continuously, until the color deepens and the rawness of the paste is cooked out, about 5 minutes. Add the coconut milk and cook until thickened, about 5 minutes more.

4. Add the stock and bring to a boil over high heat. Reduce the heat to medium and simmer, stirring occasionally, until thickened slightly and the flavors have melded, about 20 minutes. Stir in the shrimp and cook until just cooked through, about 2 minutes. Add the fish sauce, lime zest and juice, cilantro, and basil and stir to combine. Serve immediately.

Fish Tacos and All the Fixin's This is one of my favorite dishes to serve in the summer in the Hamptons. Fish tacos and fresh salsas is how I love to eat when the weather gets hot. I even make my own corn tortillas—just prepare them ahead of time along with the toppings and you'll be ready to go when guests arrive. These tacos are light but satisfying and full of flavor, and actually quite healthy, too, if you don't count all the margaritas (see page 226) that we drink to wash them down.

Serves 4 to 6

2 pounds **flaky white-fleshed fish**, such as grouper or snapper

2 teaspoons **kosher salt**

2 teaspoons **pure chile powder**, such as ancho or New Mexico chile powder

1 teaspoon **ground cumin**

1 teaspoon **ground coriander**

¼ teaspoon **freshly ground black pepper**

Canola oil

Homemade Tortillas, warmed (page 170)

Avocado Relish (page 170)

Red Cabbage Slaw (page 171)

Smoky Tomatillo Salsa (page 171)

Pickled Red Onions (page 248)

Pickled Chiles (page 249)

1. Put the fish in a baking dish. Combine the salt, chile powder, cumin, coriander, and pepper in a small bowl. Season both sides of the fish with the spice mixture and let sit at room temperature for 15 minutes.

2. Preheat the oven to 400°F.

3. Heat a few tablespoons of oil in a large cast-iron pan over high heat until it begins to shimmer. Add the fish, skin-side down, and cook until the skin is golden brown, about 4 minutes. Flip the fish, transfer the pan to the oven, and bake until just firm and cooked to medium well doneness, about 12 minutes; the fish should flake easily when tested with a fork. Remove from the oven and transfer to a cutting board. Let rest for 5 minutes (it will continue to cook), then flake into bite-size pieces with the fork.

4. Lay the tortillas on a flat surface. Spread a few tablespoons of the avocado relish on the tortillas, top with a few forkfuls of slaw and several pieces of the fish. Drizzle with the tomatillo salsa and top with pickled onions and chiles. Serve immediately.

(recipe continues)

Homemade Tortillas

Makes about 14 tortillas

2 cups **masa harina**

1 teaspoon **kosher salt**

1½ cups **hot water** (hot tap water is fine)

1. Cut a zip-top bag open along the sides. Open a tortilla press and lay the opened bag on top. (The plastic bag can be reused indefinitely; just wipe it clean of any dough after each use.)

2. Mix the masa harina and salt together in a large bowl. Pour in the hot water and stir to combine.

3. Using your hands, knead the dough for a minute or two in the bowl. The dough is ready when it's smooth and no longer sticky, and easily forms a ball in your hand. It should feel a bit "springy," like Play-Doh. Cover the dough with a damp paper towel and let rest at room temperature for 30 minutes.

4. Preheat the oven to 200°F.

5. Measure out 1-ounce balls (about the size of a golf ball) of the dough. Place a ball of dough on the plastic-covered tortilla press in the middle of the bottom plate. Fold the other side of the plastic bag over the top of the dough. Bring the top of the press down over the dough, then press with the handle to flatten the dough to about ⅛ inch thick. If the tortilla doesn't look quite even after pressing, or if you'd like it a little thinner, rotate the tortilla in the plastic and gently re-press.

6. Heat a cast-iron skillet over medium heat. Cook each tortilla in the pan until lightly golden brown on both sides, about 1 minute per side. Immediately stack on a sheet of aluminum foil, tightly wrap, and keep warm in the oven while you cook the remaining tortillas.

Avocado Relish

Makes about 1 quart

4 ripe **Hass avocados**, halved and pitted

¼ cup finely chopped **red onion**

1 or 2 **jalapeños** (depending on how spicy you like it), finely diced

Juice of 2 limes

1 teaspoon **kosher salt**

¼ teaspoon **freshly ground black pepper**

⅓ cup finely chopped fresh **cilantro leaves**

Combine the avocado, onion, jalapeños, lime juice, salt, and pepper in a large bowl and coarsely chop using a fork (leave some texture—do not overmix). Fold in the cilantro. Cover the surface of the relish with plastic wrap and refrigerate until ready to serve, up to 4 hours.

Smoky Tomatillo Salsa

Makes about 1½ cups

8 large **tomatillos**, husked, scrubbed, and quartered

1 small **red onion**, chopped

1 large **jalapeño**, chopped

5 **garlic cloves**, smashed

3 tablespoons **canola oil**

Kosher salt and **freshly ground black pepper**

1 canned **chipotle chile in adobo sauce**, chopped

½ cup fresh **cilantro leaves**

Juice of limes, plus more as needed

Clover honey (optional)

1. Preheat the oven to 400°F.

2. Combine the tomatillos, onion, jalapeño, and garlic in a large bowl. Toss with the oil and season with salt and pepper. Transfer to a baking sheet and roast until the vegetables are soft and lightly charred, about 30 minutes, stirring once.

3. Transfer the vegetables to a food processor and add the chipotle, cilantro, and lime juice. Process until smooth; season with salt and pepper. Taste and add more lime juice and honey, if needed, to round out the flavors. Scrape into a bowl and let sit at room temperature while you prepare the rest of the meal. The salsa can be made up to 1 day in advance and stored, tightly covered, in the refrigerator; bring to room temperature before serving.

Red Cabbage Slaw

Makes 1½ quarts

¼ cup **mayonnaise**, such as Hellman's

¼ cup **cider vinegar**

1 tablespoon **sugar**

½ teaspoon **celery salt**

1 teaspoon **kosher salt**

¼ teaspoon **freshly ground black pepper**

½ small head **red cabbage**, finely shredded

Whisk together the mayonnaise, vinegar, sugar, celery salt, kosher salt, and pepper in a large bowl until combined. Add the cabbage and stir to combine. Cover and refrigerate for at least 30 minutes and up to 8 hours before serving.

Steamed Mussels, Three Ways

I love steamed mussels, as they are quick, easy, flavorful, and versatile. There are so many ways to switch up the flavors, and here are three of my favorites.

Mussels in Green Curry

Serves 2 as an appetizer

This is probably my favorite way to eat mussels. I am a lover of all things curry, and green curry—with its fresh green chiles, lemongrass, makrut lime leaves, and creamy coconut milk—is that perfect combination of spicy and sweet. Green curry just happens to pair really well with seafood, too. I love serving this with Crispy Coconut-Scallion Rice (page 105) or bread.

2 tablespoons **canola oil**

1 (4-ounce) can **Maesri green curry paste**

1 (14.5-ounce) can **unsweetened coconut milk**

1 tablespoon **fish sauce**, plus more as needed

2 pounds **mussels**, scrubbed

Finely grated **zest and juice of 1 lime**, plus more lime juice as needed

¼ cup chopped fresh **Thai or Italian basil**

1. Heat the oil in a large stockpot or Dutch oven over high heat until it begins to shimmer. Add the curry paste and cook, stirring continuously, until the color deepens and the raw taste has been cooked out, about 5 minutes. Add the coconut milk, bring to a boil, and cook until the mixture has reduced by half and thickened. Add ½ cup water and the fish sauce and mix until combined.

2. Stir in the mussels, making sure to coat them all with the liquid, cover, and cook, shaking the pan a few times, until all the mussels open, about 5 minutes. Remove the mussels with a slotted spoon and transfer to a large shallow bowl, discarding any that have not opened.

3. Bring the broth back to a simmer and cook for a few minutes, until slightly reduced. Add the lime zest and juice, taste for seasoning, and add more lime juice or fish sauce if needed. Stir in the basil.

4. Pour the sauce over the mussels and serve immediately.

(recipe continues)

Moules Marinières

Serves 2 as an appetizer

I like eating these, probably the most classic version from France, as an appetizer with crusty bread to soak up all the delicious, briny liquid or serving them over pasta for a really quick late-night dinner. If you're making it a pasta dish, mix a pound of cooked spaghetti into the broth in the pan in the last step. Stir in the mussels and serve with extra lemon wedges on the side.

2 tablespoons **olive oil**

4 **shallots**, finely diced

Kosher salt

2 **garlic cloves**, chopped to a paste with the side of a chef's knife and ¼ teapoon kosher salt

1 cup **dry white wine**

1 cup **Shrimp Stock** (page 239), Fish Stock (page 237), or lobster stock

3 sprigs **thyme**

3 pounds **mussels**, scrubbed

6 tablespoons (¾ stick) cold **unsalted butter**, cut into tablespoons

Finely grated **zest of 1 lemon**

Freshly ground black pepper

¼ cup chopped fresh **flat-leaf parsley leaves**

Crusty, warm **French baguette** (optional)

1. Heat the oil in a large stockpot or Dutch oven over medium-high heat until it begins to shimmer. Add the shallots and a pinch of salt and cook until soft, about 5 minutes. Add the garlic and cook for 30 seconds. Add the wine and cook until reduced by half, about 5 minutes.

2. Add the stock and thyme and bring to a boil. Stir in the mussels, making sure they are coated with the stock and shallots. Cover and cook until all the mussels have opened, about 5 minutes. Remove the mussels with a slotted spoon and transfer to a large shallow bowl, discarding any that have not opened.

3. Bring the cooking liquid back to a boil and begin whisking in the cold butter, piece by piece, until the sauce begins to thicken. Stir in the lemon zest and season with salt and pepper.

4. Pour the broth over the mussels and garnish with the parsley. Serve with bread on the side.

Mussels with Ale and Mustard

Serves 2 as an appetizer

I am on record a million times saying that mustard is my favorite condiment, so any time I can sneak it into a dish, I will, and mussels are no exception. I love the rich, earthy taste that beer adds to soups and broths, but just like when using wine, the final product depends on the quality of beer you start with, so choose wisely.

2 tablespoons **canola oil**

1 tablespoon **unsalted butter**

1 medium **Spanish onion**, halved and thinly sliced

1 small **fennel bulb**, thinly sliced, plus ¼ cup fronds, chopped and reserved

1 **jalapeño**, finely diced

2 **garlic cloves**, chopped to a paste with the side of a chef's knife and ¼ teapoon kosher salt

1 cup **pale ale** or lager

2 pounds **mussels**, scrubbed

2 teaspoons **Dijon mustard**

Crusty, warm **French baguette**

1. Heat the oil and butter in a large stockpot or Dutch oven over high heat until the butter has melted and the mixture begins to shimmer. Add the onion and sliced fennel and cook, stirring occasionally, until soft, about 5 minutes. Add the jalapeño and garlic and cook for 30 seconds.

2. Add the beer and bring to a boil. Stir in the mussels, cover the pot, and cook, shaking the pot a few times, until all the mussels have opened. Remove the mussels with a slotted spoon and transfer to a large shallow bowl, discarding any that have not opened.

3. Bring the cooking liquid back to a boil and cook until slightly reduced, about 4 minutes. Remove from the heat and whisk in the mustard and the fennel fronds.

4. Pour the broth over the mussels and serve with bread on the side.

Crispy Soft-Shell Crabs with Harissa Vinaigrette

If I am serving grouper with tomatoes (see page 179) in August, then I am serving this in June and July when soft-shell crabs are at their best. You can grill these soft shells, too: just brush with canola, season with salt and pepper, and grill over high heat for about 4 minutes per side.

Serves 4

HARISSA VINAIGRETTE

½ cup **red wine vinegar**

2 tablespoons **harissa**

2 teaspoons **Dijon mustard**

½ teaspoon **kosher salt**

⅛ teaspoon **freshly ground black pepper**

1 cup **blended oil** (equal parts canola and extra-virgin olive oil)

1 teaspoon **clover honey**

CRABS

8 medium **soft-shell crabs**, cleaned and rinsed with cold water

4 cups **canola oil**

Kosher salt and **freshly ground black pepper**

2 cups **rice flour**

¼ cup **capers**, drained and coarsely chopped

¼ cup chopped fresh **flat-leaf parsley leaves**

TIP How should you dispose of frying oil properly? Never put oil, hot or cold, down your drain. It will clog the pipes and create a plumbing nightmare. After you are done frying, let the oil cool completely, then transfer it to a large plastic bag or zip-top bag. Seal the bag, put it in a larger trash bag, and put it out with the garbage.

1. **Make the vinaigrette:** Whisk together the vinegar, harissa, mustard, salt, and pepper in a medium bowl. While whisking, slowly drizzle in the oil and whisk until emulsified. Whisk in the honey until combined.

2. **Cook the crabs:** Preheat the oven to 300°F.

3. Line a large baking sheet with several layers of paper towels, put the crabs on the baking sheet in an even layer, and top with more paper towels to blot dry. (Getting the crabs as dry as possible before frying is important, because water and hot oil do not mix. You are still going to get some popping, so do not be alarmed, but drying them as much as you can will help.)

4. Set a wire rack over a baking sheet and place it nearby. Heat the oil in a large Dutch oven over medium heat until it reaches 350°F on a deep-fry thermometer.

5. Season the crabs on both sides with salt and pepper. Put ½ cup of the flour in a shallow dish and season with salt and pepper. Whisk together the remaining 1½ cups flour and 1½ cups cold water in a large bowl and season with salt and pepper. Dredge the crabs in the flour on both sides and tap off any excess. Dip them into the batter and let any excess drip off.

6. Working in batches of two, add the crabs to the hot oil and fry until golden brown and crispy, turning once, about 4 minutes total. Transfer to the rack on the baking sheet and immediately season with a touch of salt. Keep warm in the oven. Repeat to cook the remaining crabs.

7. Drizzle some of the vinaigrette onto a serving platter. Place the fried crabs on top and drizzle with a bit more vinaigrette. Combine the capers and parsley in a small bowl and sprinkle over the top. Serve immediately with the remaining vinaigrette on the side.

Grilled Grouper with Balsam Farms Tomatoes and Avocado

I serve this about once a week during the month of August, sometimes twice. I can't get enough summer tomatoes from my local farm stand (Balsam Farms), which is about a half mile from my home in the Hamptons. All summer I am blessed with a bounty of fruits, vegetables, and herbs, along with the freshest fish from Citarella in East Hampton—it's really simplistic perfection at its best.

Serves 4 to 6

1½ pounds **assorted summer tomatoes**, sliced, diced, or halved (depending on the size)

¼ cup **extra-virgin olive oil**, plus more as needed

1 teaspoon **kosher salt**, plus more as needed

1½ pounds fresh **grouper**

¼ cup **canola oil**

Freshly ground black pepper

2 **Hass avocados**, pitted, peeled, and diced

½ cup chopped fresh **dill**

¼ cup fresh **basil** or flat-leaf parsley leaves, for garnish

1. Combine the tomatoes, olive oil, and salt in a large bowl and let sit at room temperature until ready to serve.

2. Heat a grill to high.

3. Brush the fish on both sides with the canola oil and season with salt and pepper. Grill until golden brown and charred on both sides and just cooked through, about 4 minutes per side, depending on the thickness.

4. Just before serving, add the avocados and dill to the tomatoes and season with more salt and some pepper. Transfer the fish to a platter and top with the tomato mixture. Drizzle with more olive oil, garnish with the basil, and serve.

Oyster Shooters

Oyster shooters are a fun, tasty cocktail–hors d'oeuvre hybrid. Drop a plump, freshly shucked oyster into a shot glass, top off with booze, and tip it back. I started serving them at Bobby Flay Steak in Atlantic City, where the mood is festive and the diners are often open to excess. This shooter takes a briny fresh oyster and pairs it with a "shot" of smoky, vodka-spiked cocktail sauce—think of it as a concentrated Bloody Mary.

Makes 16 shooters

COCKTAIL SAUCE

⅔ cup **ketchup**

3 tablespoons prepared **horseradish**, drained

3 tablespoons **vodka**

1 tablespoon puréed **canned chipotle chile in adobo sauce** (see Note, page 60)

2 teaspoons **Worcestershire sauce**

Juice of ½ small lemon

¼ teaspoon **kosher** salt

¼ teaspoon **freshly ground black pepper**

16 **oysters**, shucked

Green Tabasco sauce

Finely grated **lime zest**

1. **Make the cocktail sauce:** Whisk together the ketchup, horseradish, vodka, chipotle purée, Worcestershire, lemon juice, salt, and pepper in a medium bowl. Cover and refrigerate for at least 30 minutes and up to 1 day.

2. For each shooter, slip 1 oyster into a double shot glass and top with a heaping tablespoon of the cocktail sauce, a splash of green Tabasco, and some lime zest. Serve immediately.

Red Snapper with Ancho Chile Broth and Posole

The double technique of pan-roasting and steaming gives you the best of both worlds when it comes to cooking fish. Searing it first in a pan gives the fish texture, then poaching it in the broth infuses it with flavor while keeping the flesh moist.

Serves 4

2 dried **ancho chiles**

2 dried **pasilla chiles**

1 whole dried **chile de árbol**

Boiling water, as needed

4 tablespoons **canola oil**

1 medium **Spanish onion**, halved and thinly sliced

5 **garlic cloves**, chopped

6 cups **Fish Stock** (page 237)

1 teaspoon **dried oregano**

5 sprigs **cilantro**

1 **bay leaf**

1¼ pounds center-cut **red snapper fillet** (or substitute grouper or halibut)

1 (15-ounce) can **hominy**, drained, rinsed well, and drained again

1 ripe **Hass avocado**, pitted, peeled, and diced

1 cup finely shredded **green cabbage**

¼ cup fresh **cilantro leaves**

4 **lime wedges**

1. Heat a pan over medium heat until smoking. Add the chiles and toast on both sides until fragrant and deeper red in color, about 1 minute per side. When cool enough to handle, remove the stems and seeds and transfer the chiles to a medium bowl. Cover with boiling water by 2 inches. Let soak until soft, about 30 minutes.

2. Transfer the chiles and ¼ cup of their soaking liquid to a blender. Blend until a smooth paste forms, adding more soaking liquid, a few tablespoons at a time, if needed to loosen it.

3. Heat 2 tablespoons of the oil in a large high-sided sauté pan over high heat. Add the onion and cook until soft, about 4 minutes. Add the garlic and cook for 1 minute. Add the chile paste and cook for 1 minute. Add the stock, oregano, cilantro, and bay leaf and bring to a boil over high heat. Reduce the heat to medium-low and simmer, stirring occasionally, for 30 minutes. Transfer the broth to a large bowl and let cool for 15 minutes. Working in batches, transfer to a food processor or blender and process until smooth.

4. Return the pan to the stove and heat the remaining 2 tablespoons oil over high heat. Season the fish with salt and pepper on both sides. Add the fish to the hot oil and sear until golden brown on both sides, about 4 minutes per side. Transfer to a plate. Add the hominy to the pan and cook, stirring continuously, until golden brown and crispy, about 5 minutes. Return the broth and the fish to the pan and bring to a boil. Reduce the heat to low, cover, and cook until the fish is just cooked through, about 8 minutes.

5. Remove the fish from the soup with a slotted spoon and divide it into four portions. Place each portion in a shallow bowl and ladle the broth over the top. Garnish with the avocado, cabbage, cilantro, and lime wedges and serve.

Slow-Roasted Salmon with Farro and Greens

Everyone thinks that salmon has to either be poached or cooked over high heat, but letting it bake slowly in the oven allows the salmon to cook in its own fat and yields a tender, moist piece of fish every time. Farro is an ancient grain full of protein and fiber, with a nutty flavor and chewy texture that holds up to the double cooking it gets in this dish.

Serves 4

VINAIGRETTE

1 small **shallot**, very finely chopped

¼ cup fresh **lemon juice**

1 tablespoon **Dijon mustard**

1 teaspoon **clover honey**

Kosher salt and **freshly ground black pepper**

½ cup **olive oil**

Canola oil, plus more for greasing

2 tablespoons **capers**, drained, rinsed, and patted dry

1 cup **farro**

Kosher salt and **freshly ground black pepper**

1 **garlic clove**, thinly sliced

1 bunch small **mustard greens**, ribs and stems removed, leaves coarsely chopped

1 teaspoon **clover honey**

4 (6-ounce) skinless **salmon fillets**

1. **Make the vinaigrette:** Whisk together the shallot, lemon juice, mustard, and honey in a small bowl; season with salt and pepper. While whisking, slowly drizzle in the olive oil and whisk until emulsified. Taste for seasoning and adjust if needed.

2. Heat ¼ cup canola oil in a small saucepan over medium-high heat until it shimmers. Add the capers and cook until opened and crisp, about 30 seconds. Use a slotted spoon to transfer to a plate lined with paper towels. Set aside.

3. Put the farro in a pot and add 2 cups cold water, 1 teaspoon salt, and ¼ teaspoon pepper. Bring to a boil over high heat. Reduce the heat to low, cover, and cook until the farro is tender and all the liquid has been absorbed, about 40 minutes. Transfer the farro to a large bowl and add 2 tablespoons of the vinaigrette; toss to coat.

4. Preheat the oven to 250°F. Lightly oil a large *cazuela* or 9 × 13-inch baking dish.

5. Heat the 1 tablespoon canola oil in a large skillet over medium-high heat until it begins to shimmer. Add the garlic and cook, stirring, until fragrant, about 30 seconds. Add the mustard greens and cook, tossing, until slightly wilted, about 1 minute. Add ¼ cup water; season with salt and pepper. Cook, tossing, until the greens are completely wilted, about 3 minutes. Stir in the honey. Transfer to the bowl with the farro and stir to combine. Transfer the mixture to the prepared baking dish and set aside.

6. Season the salmon with salt and pepper on both sides; arrange the fillets over the farro mixture and drizzle with olive oil. Bake until the salmon is opaque in the center, 30 to 35 minutes. Remove from the oven and immediately drizzle with the remaining vinaigrette, top with the capers, and serve.

Swordfish with Plum Agrodolce

This dish originated in Puglia, Italy, many years ago while I was on vacation with my business partner Laurence Kretchmer, my good friend Michael Symon, and our families. Each morning, we would go to the market and shop for dinner for that night. This is what I served on one of my nights to cook, and I honestly have been making it every summer since. If you can't find plums, nectarines will work; if you don't like swordfish, use halibut or grouper. This sauce is also really great served over pork.

Serves 4

PLUM AGRODOLCE

4 cups **red wine vinegar**

1 cup **clover honey**

3 **black plums**, halved, pitted, and chopped

Kosher salt and **freshly ground black pepper**

2 tablespoons **canola oil**

4 (1-inch-thick) **swordfish fillets** (about 2 pounds total)

Kosher salt and **freshly ground black pepper**

1 heaping tablespoon **capers**, drained

2 **black plums**, pitted and thinly sliced

2 tablespoons chopped fresh **mint leaves**, plus more for garnish

Extra-virgin olive oil, for garnish

1. **Make the plum agrodolce:** Add the vinegar, honey, and chopped plums to a large nonstick saucepan, bring to a boil over high heat, reduce the heat to medium, and cook until the liquid has reduced by half and the mixture has almost a saucelike consistency. Taste and season with salt and pepper. Strain through a fine-mesh strainer into a bowl and set aside; discard the solids.

2. Heat the canola oil in a large sauté pan over high heat until it begins to shimmer. Season the swordfish on both sides with salt and pepper. Add the fish to the hot oil and sear until both sides are golden brown, about 3 minutes per side. Transfer to a plate.

3. Add the agrodolce to the pan and bring to a simmer over low heat. Add the capers and three-quarters of the sliced plums and cook until the plums soften, about 2 minutes per side. Return the swordfish to the pan, cover, and cook until the swordfish is just cooked through, about 5 minutes. Season with salt and pepper and add the mint.

4. Serve the swordfish topped with a few slices of the plums and a bit more fresh mint and drizzled with a few teaspoons of extra-virgin olive oil.

Spanish-Style Shrimp and Grits

Last year, I did a pop-up brunch for one of my restaurants, Gato, taking classic brunch items and giving them a Mediterranean spin. This dish—the shrimp seasoned with savory, smoky Spanish spices and punctuated with salty serrano ham, served atop a bowl of Manchego cheese–enriched grits—is one of the best of those dishes. These grits may not have made Gato's menu, but you'll be so very happy they made it into this book.

Serves 4 to 6

3 tablespoons **sweet Spanish paprika**

1 tablespoon **ancho chile powder**

2 teaspoons **ground coriander**

2 teaspoons **ground fennel**

2 teaspoons **dry mustard**

2 teaspoons **kosher salt**

½ teaspoon **freshly ground black pepper**

1 pound large **shrimp** (21 to 25 count), peeled and deveined

2 tablespoons plus ¼ cup **canola oil**

1 (6-ounce) piece **serrano ham**, diced

3 **garlic cloves**, sliced

Pinch of **crushed red pepper flakes**

¼ cup **dry white wine**

1 (15-ounce) can **plum tomatoes**, with their juices

1 tablespoon **aged sherry vinegar**

¼ cup chopped fresh **flat-leaf parsley leaves**

Manchego Grits (page 189), warm

3 **scallions**, green and pale green parts only, thinly sliced

1. Combine the paprika, ancho chile powder, coriander, fennel, mustard, salt, and pepper in a small bowl. Put the shrimp in a large bowl, add the spice rub, and toss to coat. Let sit while you start the sauce.

2. Line a plate with paper towels. Heat 2 tablespoons of the oil in a large high-sided sauté pan over high heat until it begins to shimmer. Add the ham and cook until golden brown on both sides, about 4 minutes. Remove with a slotted spoon and transfer to the prepared plate.

3. In the same pan, heat 2 tablespoons of the oil over high heat until it begins to shimmer. Working in batches, add half the shrimp and cook until a crust forms on both sides, about 1 minute per side. Transfer to a large plate. Repeat with the remaining 2 tablespoons oil and shrimp; transfer the second batch of cooked shrimp to the plate with the first.

4. Add the garlic to the pan and cook until soft and lightly golden brown, about 1 minute. Add the red pepper flakes and cook for 10 seconds more. Add the wine and cook, stirring a few times, until completely reduced, about 2 minutes. Add the tomatoes and cook until they begin to soften, about 10 minutes. Using a potato masher, coarsely crush the tomatoes directly in the pan. Cook until the sauce thickens, about 10 minutes more. Return the shrimp to the pan and cook, stirring once, until just heated through, about 2 minutes. Remove the pan from the heat and stir in the vinegar and parsley.

5. Scrape the grits into a large shallow bowl. Top with the shrimp and sauce, garnish with the scallions, and serve.

(recipe continues)

Manchego Grits

Makes about 4 cups

2 cups **whole milk**

Kosher salt and **freshly ground black pepper**

1 cup coarse **cornmeal**

1 cup coarsely grated **Manchego cheese**

¼ cup grated **cotija cheese**

2 tablespoons **unsalted butter**, cut into pieces

NOTE While I prefer to use coarse cornmeal in this dish because I just like the texture better, you can substitute polenta or grits in this recipe. Just cook according to the directions on the package.

1. Combine the milk and 2 cups water in a large saucepan and season with 2 teaspoons salt and ¼ teaspoon pepper. Bring to a boil over high heat. While whisking, slowly add the cornmeal and whisk until the mixture begins to thicken, about 2 minutes. Reduce the heat to medium and cook, whisking occasionally, until the texture is silky and soft, about 35 minutes. Add additional water if the grits become too thick before they're cooked through.

2. Right before serving, whisk in the cheeses and butter until smooth. Taste and season with more salt and pepper, if needed. Keep warm until ready to serve.

DESSERTS

Historically, dessert has not been my strong suit—that's why I've always had excellent pastry chefs in my restaurants! But if you love to entertain as I do, and if you must end your meal on a sweet note—as I definitely do—then at some point, you have to tackle the flour, butter, and sugar head-on and cultivate a repertoire of go-to desserts. Some recipes, such as the Master Recipe for Shortcakes, Crostatas, and Cobblers (page 192) will do triple-duty: just master one simple dough and with a few different fruits and techniques tweaks, you'll have delicious, homey desserts for days. I have no problem answering "Pie, please," if a friend asks what they can contribute to a casual meal, but there's something to be said for pulling out all the stops and making something from scratch for your guests. The fact that I can pull off a No-Bake Chocolate Hazelnut Crema Catalana (page 210) to complete a Spanish-influenced menu is something that I'm pretty proud of, if I do say so myself.

Master Recipe for Shortcakes, Crostatas, and Cobblers

For someone like me who really does not enjoy baking, shortcakes, crostatas, and cobblers are my go-to desserts. They're easy and can be made year-round by using frozen fruit when fresh is out of season. Some of my favorite combinations are rhubarb and blackberry, white peach and raspberry, blueberry and nectarine, and of course strawberry when in season. I have found that one dough, handled differently for each application, works perfectly, thus making me "enjoy" baking just a bit more.

Shortcakes

Makes 4 shortcakes

Basic Dough (page 194)

Heavy cream for brushing

Granulated or turbinado **sugar**, for sprinkling

Fresh fruit (such as berries or sliced stone fruit), for serving

Whipped cream, for serving

1. Preheat the oven to 400°F. Line a baking sheet with parchment paper.

2. Remove the dough from the refrigerator and place on a floured surface. Roll out the dough to 1-inch thickness. Using a biscuit cutter or glass, cut out 3-inch rounds and transfer them to the prepared baking sheet. Brush the tops with cream and sprinkle each with ½ teaspoon of sugar.

3. Bake until lightly golden brown, about 15 minutes. Serve with fruit and whipped cream.

Crostata

Makes one 9-inch crostata

Basic Dough (page 194)

Cooked Fruit Filling (page 195)

Granulated or turbinado **sugar**, for sprinkling

1. Preheat the oven to 375°F. Line a baking sheet with parchment paper or aluminum foil.

2. On a floured surface, roll the dough into a 12-inch round, ¼ inch thick. Transfer the dough round to the prepared baking sheet. Fill the center with the fruit filling, leaving a 2-inch border. Gently fold the border over the fruit, leaving the center exposed, and pleat the border to make a circle. Sprinkle the sugar evenly over the dough.

3. Bake until the crust is golden brown and the fruit is bubbling, about 30 minutes. Let cool for 10 minutes before slicing.

4. Serve warm or at room temperature.

(recipe continues)

Cobbler

Makes one 9-inch cobbler

Basic Dough (recipe follows)

Unsalted butter, for greasing the pan

Macerated Fruit Filling (recipe follows)

2 tablespoons **whole milk** or heavy cream

2 tablespoons **sugar**

Vanilla ice cream or whipped cream, for serving (optional)

1. Preheat the oven to 350°F. Lightly butter a 9-inch baking dish. Line a baking sheet with parchment paper or aluminum foil.

2. Fill the prepared baking dish with the fruit filling and set aside.

3. On a floured surface, roll out the dough into a 9-inch square; trim off and discard the excess dough. Place the dough over the fruit in the baking dish and tuck in the excess. Place the dish on the prepared baking sheet. Brush the top of the dough with the milk and sprinkle the sugar evenly over the dough. Using a paring knife, make a few slices into the crust.

4. Bake until the crust is golden brown and the fruit is bubbling, about 40 minutes. Remove from the oven and let rest for at least 15 minutes before serving.

5. Serve in bowls with vanilla ice cream or whipped cream, if desired.

Basic Dough

Makes enough dough for 4 shortcakes or one 9-inch cobbler or crostata

1½ cups **all-purpose flour**, plus more for dusting

3 tablespoons **pure sugar**

1½ teaspoons **baking powder**

½ teaspoon **baking soda**

¼ teaspoon **kosher salt**

3 tablespoons cold **unsalted butter**, cut into small cubes

¼ cup plus 1 tablespoon very cold **buttermilk**

¼ cup plus 1 tablespoon very cold **heavy cream**

1. Combine the flour, sugar, baking powder, baking soda, and salt in a large bowl. Cut in the butter using your fingers, two knives, or a pastry cutter until the mixture resembles coarse meal. Slowly add the buttermilk and cream and gently mix, using your fingers or a fork, until the mixture just comes together. (Alternatively, combine the flour, sugar, baking powder, baking soda, salt, and butter in a food processor and pulse a few times. Add the buttermilk and heavy cream and pulse until the dough just comes together.)

2. Transfer the dough to a lightly floured surface and sprinkle a bit more flour on top. Lightly flatten the dough using a rolling pin or your hands, fold it over, and flatten again. Fold it over once more, then wrap in plastic wrap and refrigerate until chilled, at least 30 minutes and up to 2 days.

Macerated Fruit Filling

Makes enough for one 9-inch cobbler

6 cups sliced fresh or frozen (not thawed) **fruits**, such as stone fruit, berries, or pitted cherries

¼ to ½ cup **sugar** (depending on the sweetness and ripeness of the fruit)

3 to 4 tablespoons **cornstarch**

1 teaspoon finely grated **lemon, lime,** or **orange zest**

Pinch of **kosher salt**

Combine the fruit and sugar in a large bowl and let macerate for 15 minutes. Add the cornstarch (3 tablespoons for fresh fruit or 4 tablespoons for frozen fruit), citrus zest, and the salt and stir well to combine.

TIPS
- If using frozen fruit, do not thaw first.
- Lemon or orange zest is great for berries, rhubarb, and cherries; orange goes well with peaches; and lime is perfect for mangoes.

Cooked Fruit Filling

Makes enough for one 9-inch crostata

3 cups diced fresh or frozen (not thawed) **fruit**, such as mangoes, peaches, whole blackberries, or blueberries

3 to 6 tablespoons **sugar** (depending on the sweetness and ripeness of the fruit)

½ teaspoon **cornstarch**, mixed with 1 teaspoon cold water

½ teaspoon finely grated **lemon** or **lime zest**

1 tablespoon fresh **lemon** or **lime juice**

Pinch of **kosher salt**

Combine the fruit and sugar in a large bowl and let sit at room temperature until the juices begin to release, about 30 minutes. Transfer the mixture to a saucepan and bring to a boil over high heat. Add the cornstarch slurry, bring to a boil, and cook until the mixture thickens, about 1 minute. Remove from the heat and stir in the citrus zest and juice and salt.

NOTE It is my belief that since crostatas are relatively small in size and the dough is rolled so thin, their short bake time is not long enough for the fruit to cook through and for the juices to thicken. So when I make crostatas, I like to give the fruit a head start by making it into an almost jam-like filling to begin with. If you are short on time and you have jam in your refrigerator, that will work as a filling, too! Just use 1 cup prepared jam (raspberry, apricot, peach, blackberry) mixed with 2 teaspoons fresh lemon juice.

Gluten-Free Peanut Butter Sandwich Cookies

Josephine Pacquing, my pastry chef at Bar Americain for years, created these cookies for our cookie plate at BA, and they are always a hit with the diners. I love that the cookies just happen to be gluten-free, too, considering how many of my friends have gone that route today, whether for health reasons or simply by choice.

Makes about 48 sandwich cookies

COOKIES

18 ounces **smooth peanut butter** (do *not* use natural; we recommend Skippy)

½ cup (1 stick) **unsalted butter**, at room temperature

1½ cups **granulated sugar**

1½ cups packed **light brown sugar**

2½ teaspoons **baking soda**

⅛ teaspoon **fine sea salt**

4 large **eggs**

1 teaspoon **pure vanilla extract**

6 cups **quick-cooking oats** (check the label to make sure it's gluten-free)

FILLING

8 ounces **smooth peanut butter** (do *not* use natural; we recommend Skippy)

1 (8-ounce) package **cream cheese**, at room temperature

½ cup (1 stick) **unsalted butter**, at room temperature

8 ounces **confectioners' sugar**, sifted

1 tablespoon **pure vanilla extract**

1. **Make the cookies:** Using a handheld mixer, beat the peanut butter and butter in a large bowl on high speed until smooth. Add both sugars, the baking soda, and the salt and mix until combined.

2. Add the eggs one at a time and beat until incorporated. Add the vanilla and beat until combined. Fold in the oats. Cover and refrigerate the mixture until slightly chilled, at least 30 minutes and up to 2 hours.

3. Preheat the oven to 350°F. Line a baking sheet with parchment paper.

4. Working in batches, use a small ice cream scoop (about 1 heaping tablespoon), spoon the dough onto the prepared baking sheets, spacing the cookies 2 inches apart and flattening the tops slightly. Bake until lightly golden brown and just set, about 10 minutes. Let cool on the baking sheets on a wire rack for 5 minutes. Transfer to the rack and let cool completely before filling. Repeat with the remaining dough.

5. **Make the filling:** Using a handheld mixer, beat the peanut butter, cream cheese, and butter in a medium bowl on high speed until smooth. Add the confectioners' sugar and vanilla and mix until smooth.

6. Put half the cooled cookies flat-side up on a flat surface. Spread the filling over the cookies, then top with the remaining cookies, with the flat sides against the filling, to form sandwiches.

Gingerbread and Lemon Curd Trifle with Blackberry Sauce

This is my go-to Christmas dinner dessert. It's a showstopper and the best part is that it is so easy. You are really only making a gingerbread cake. The rest of the work is opening a jar of lemon curd, whipping some heavy cream, and puréeing some berries. Your guests will think that you worked for days on it—let them keep thinking that. You can also just sub in prepared pound cake or angel food cake for the homemade gingerbread to make it even easier, but just as tasty.

Serves 8

GINGERBREAD CAKE

Nonstick cooking spray

3 cups **all-purpose flour**

2 tablespoons **ground ginger**

2 teaspoons **baking soda**

1¼ teaspoons **ground cinnamon**

¾ teaspoon **ground cloves**

½ teaspoon freshly grated **nutmeg**

¼ teaspoon **kosher salt**

3 tablespoons minced **crystallized ginger**

10 tablespoons (1¼ sticks) **unsalted butter**, at room temperature

1 cup packed **light brown sugar**

3 large **eggs**

1 cup **molasses**

1 cup **boiling water**

2½ teaspoons finely grated **lemon zest**

1. Make the gingerbread cake: Position a rack in the center of the oven and preheat the oven to 350°F. Spray an 18 × 13-inch rimmed baking sheet with nonstick spray. Line the bottom of the sheet with parchment paper and spray the paper with nonstick spray as well.

2. Sift together the flour, ground ginger, baking soda, cinnamon, cloves, nutmeg, and salt into a medium bowl. Mix in the crystallized ginger. Set aside.

3. Using a handheld mixer, beat the butter and brown sugar in a large bowl on high speed, stopping and scraping down the bottom and sides of the bowl a few times, until light and fluffy, about 5 minutes. Beat in the eggs one at a time, scraping down the bowl a few times. Gradually beat in the molasses, followed by the boiling water. Mix in the lemon zest. Gradually mix in the dry ingredients.

4. Transfer the batter to the prepared baking sheet. Bake until a tester inserted into the center of the gingerbread comes out clean, 20 to 25 minutes. Let cool on the baking sheet on a wire rack for 15 minutes.

5. Meanwhile, make the lemon curd filling: Using a handheld mixer, beat the cream, granulated sugar, and vanilla in a large bowl until soft peaks form. Place the lemon curd in a large bowl. Fold in half of the whipped cream until combined. Reserve the remaining whipped cream for topping the trifle. If not using the filling and whipped cream immediately, cover and refrigerate until ready to use.

2 cups very cold **heavy cream**

2 tablespoons **granulated sugar**

½ teaspoon **pure vanilla extract**

2 (11-ounce) jars prepared
lemon curd

BLACKBERRY SAUCE

2 pints fresh **blackberries**

¼ cup **granulated sugar**, or more,
depending on the sweetness of the
berries

Pinch of **kosher salt**

2 tablespoons **framboise** (raspberry)
liqueur

1 tablespoon fresh **lemon juice**

6. Make the blackberry sauce: Combine the blackberries, granulated sugar, and salt in a medium saucepan and cook over high heat, stirring a few times, until the berries are soft and the sugar has dissolved, about 7 minutes. Carefully transfer the mixture to a blender and blend until smooth. Pour through a strainer into a bowl. Stir in the framboise and lemon juice. Set aside until ready to use.

7. Run a knife between the cooled gingerbread cake and the sides of the baking sheet. Turn the gingerbread out onto the rack and peel off the parchment paper. Let cool, then cut into 1-inch cubes.

8. In a trifle bowl, start with an even layer of gingerbread cubes. Top with one-third of the lemon curd filling, then one-third of the blackberry sauce. Repeat these layers twice more. Top with the reserved whipped cream. (Alternatively, layer the gingerbread cubes, filling, sauce, and whipped cream in large individual wine goblets.) Cover and refrigerate for at least 4 hours or up to overnight before serving.

Chocolate Chip Cookies

This is my favorite chocolate chip cookie (well, other than Jacques Torres's) and I always have the dough in my fridge or freezer. Did you know that the longer the dough sits, the better the cookie is? If you are making these and planning on eating them right away, start at least 1 day and preferably up to 3 days in advance and let the dough sit in the fridge so the flavors intensify.

Makes about 48 cookies

2 cups plus 3 tablespoons **all-purpose flour**

¾ teaspoon **kosher salt**, or ½ teaspoon fine sea salt

¾ teaspoon **baking soda**

1 cup (2 sticks) **unsalted butter**, at room temperature

1 cup **granulated sugar**

⅓ cup packed **dark brown muscovado sugar**

⅓ cup packed **light brown muscovado sugar**

2 large **eggs**

1½ teaspoons **pure vanilla extract**

1 (5-ounce) block **semisweet chocolate** (such as Callebaut), chopped into chunks

1 (5-ounce) block **milk chocolate** (such as Callebaut), chopped into chunks

1. Whisk together the flour, salt, and baking soda in a medium bowl. Set aside.

2. In the bowl of a stand mixer fitted with the paddle attachment, beat the butter on high speed until smooth, about 1 minute. Add the sugars and beat, stopping and scraping down the sides and bottom of the bowl occasionally, until light and fluffy, about 2 minutes. Add the eggs one at a time, beating each until just incorporated before adding the next. Add the vanilla and beat for a few seconds.

3. Add half the flour mixture and mix until just incorporated. Add the remaining flour mixture and again mix until just combined. Remove the bowl from the stand mixer and fold in the chocolate chunks. Cover and refrigerate for at least 1 day and (for best flavor) up to 3 days.

4. Position a rack in the center of the oven and preheat the oven to 375°F. Line baking sheets with parchment paper or silicone baking mats.

5. Using a small ice cream scoop (about 1 heaping tablespoon), spoon the dough onto the baking sheet, leaving at least 2 inches between each cookie. Bake on the center rack until the cookies are lightly golden brown and still soft in the middle, about 11 minutes. Let the cookies cool on the baking sheets for 2 minutes, then use a wide metal spatula to transfer them to a wire rack. Repeat with remaining dough. Let the cookies cool completely on the rack before serving.

My Favorite Brownie Recipe

My business assistant and cowriter, Stephanie Banyas, created this recipe for a *Throwdown* battle years ago. Though we lost the battle (it was super close), we won with this recipe—it has become the only brownie recipe that we will ever make again. If you like your brownies fudgy, not cakey, this is the one for you.

Makes 24 small or 12 large brownies

Nonstick cooking spray

1 cup (2 sticks) **unsalted butter**, cut into chunks

6 ounces high-quality **unsweetened chocolate**, coarsely chopped

2 ounces **bittersweet chocolate**, coarsely chopped

1 teaspoon **espresso powder**

4 large **eggs**

1½ cups **granulated sugar**

½ cup packed **light brown muscovado sugar**

2 teaspoons **pure vanilla extract**

¼ teaspoon **fine sea salt**

1 cup **all-purpose flour**

4 ounces **semisweet chocolate**, coarsely chopped or cut into shards

1¼ cups **chopped nuts** (such as pecans, walnuts, hazelnuts), lightly toasted (optional)

1. Position a rack in the center of the oven and preheat the oven to 325°F. Spray a 9 × 13-inch pan with nonstick spray and line with aluminum foil, leaving a 2-inch overhang.

2. Bring a medium pot of water to a boil. Combine the butter, unsweetened chocolate, bittersweet chocolate, and the espresso powder in a medium heatproof bowl. Set the bowl over the simmering water (be sure the bottom of the bowl doesn't touch the water) and heat over low heat, stirring frequently, until melted, well combined, and smooth. Remove from the heat and let cool slightly, about 5 minutes.

3. In a large bowl, whisk together the eggs, both sugars, the vanilla, and the salt until smooth. Whisk in the melted chocolate mixture until smooth. Scrape down the sides of the bowl. Whisk in the flour in two additions (the batter will be thick). Stir in the semisweet chocolate.

4. Scrape the batter into the prepared pan and smooth the top. Bake for 28 minutes, or until the top is set but still soft and the edges are puffed and just beginning to pull away from the sides of the pan. A toothpick inserted into the center will come out still *gooey*. (Be brave! *Underbaking* the brownies is one of the secrets to their fudgy texture.) Transfer the pan to a wire rack and let the brownies cool to room temperature, about 1 hour.

5. For the neatest cuts, cut the brownies while cold: Cover the pan with foil and refrigerate until chilled, about 2 hours. Using the overhanging foil as handles, lift the brownie slab out of the pan. Carefully peel off the foil and put the brownie on a large cutting board. With a large sharp knife, cut the brownies into squares and serve.

Roasted Peaches with Mascarpone, Via Carota Style

One of my favorite restaurants in New York (and America, for that matter) is Via Carota in the West Village. Owned by the chef power team of Jody Williams and Rita Sodi, the restaurant serves homemade pastas, simply grilled meats, and seasonal salads that I honestly could eat every single day of my life until the end of time. Their desserts are just as simple and delicious, and this is one of my favorite ways to end my meals there.

Serves 4

5 ripe large **peaches** (about 2½ pounds total), halved, pitted, and each half cut into thirds

¼ to ½ cup **sugar**, depending on the ripeness of the peaches

¼ cup **Amaretto**

1¼ cups **mascarpone cheese**, slightly softened (take out of refrigerator 30 minutes before serving)

½ cup sliced **almonds**, lightly toasted (optional)

1. Preheat the oven to 400°F.

2. Combine the peaches and sugar in a large bowl and gently mix to combine. Let the peaches sit until their juices begins to run, about 15 minutes. Stir in the Amaretto.

3. Transfer the peaches to a large baking dish and roast until golden brown and the edges are slightly charred, about 25 minutes, stirring once. Let cool for 10 minutes. Remove the peaches with a slotted spoon and transfer to a platter, reserving the juices in the pan.

4. Transfer the juices to a large sauté pan and cook over high heat until reduced by half. Pour the reduced liquid over the peaches.

5. Serve the peaches in bowls, with a large dollop of mascarpone on top and garnished with the almonds.

Stephie B's Banana Pudding

My assistant of twenty-three years and coauthor Stephanie Banyas developed this recipe years ago. After seeing a version of it made on TV with boxed pudding and nondairy whipped topping (not that there's anything wrong with that), she set out to create a more "homemade" version.

Serves 6 to 8

⅔ cup **pure cane sugar**

¼ cup **cornstarch**

¼ teaspoon **fine sea salt**

2½ cups **whole milk**

4 large **egg yolks**, lightly beaten

2 tablespoons **unsalted butter**, cut into pieces

1½ teaspoons **pure vanilla extract**

2 teaspoons **bourbon** (optional)

1½ cups very cold **heavy cream**

1 (8-ounce) package **cream cheese**, at room temperature

1 (14-ounce) can **sweetened condensed milk**

2 (7.25-ounce) packages **Pepperidge Farm Chessmen cookies**

4 large ripe **bananas**, cut into ¼-inch-thick slices

Sweetened freshly **whipped cream**, for serving (see Note)

NOTE For the whipped cream topping, combine 1½ cups very cold heavy cream, 3 tablespoons sugar, and 1 teaspoon vanilla extract in the bowl of a stand mixer and whip using the whisk attachment until soft peaks form.

1. Whisk together the cane sugar, cornstarch, and salt in a medium nonreactive saucepan. Slowly whisk in the milk until a smooth mixture forms. Whisk in the egg yolks until smooth. Cook over medium heat, whisking continuously, until the first large bubble forms and sputters. Reduce the heat to low and cook, whisking continuously, for 1 minute more, or until thickened. Remove from the heat and transfer the pudding to a medium bowl. Stir in the butter, vanilla, and bourbon (if using) until combined. Cover the top with plastic wrap pressed directly against the surface. Refrigerate for at least 1 hour and up to 4 hours.

2. In the bowl of a stand mixer fitted with the whisk attachment, whip the cream until soft peaks form; transfer to a separate bowl and set aside.

3. In the bowl of the stand mixer, whip the cream cheese and condensed milk until smooth. Add the vanilla pudding to the cream cheese mixture and whip until light and fluffy. Transfer to a bowl and fold in the whipped cream.

4. Line the bottom of a 9 × 13-inch baking dish with a single layer of the cookies. Top the cookies with half the banana slices. Spread half the pudding mixture evenly over the top of the bananas, making sure to completely cover the slices. Repeat with the remaining cookies, banana slices, and pudding. Cover with plastic wrap and refrigerate for at least 8 hours and up to 24 hours before serving (the pudding is best if chilled for at least 8 hours). Right before serving, spread the freshly whipped cream over the top.

Tiramisu

I love this recipe for tiramisu, and I make it often. It is simple and delicious, but it does require a bit of planning, as it needs to sit for at least 8 hours in the refrigerator to allow the flavors to meld before serving.

Serves 8

8 extra-large **egg yolks**

½ cup **sugar**

¼ cup plus 1½ tablespoons **Kahlúa**

17 ounces **mascarpone cheese**, at room temperature

6 cups **strong brewed coffee**, preferably espresso, cooled

36 **ladyfingers**, such as Savoiardi (imported Italian ladyfingers)

¼ cup good-quality **unsweetened Dutch-processed cocoa powder**

1. In the bowl of a stand mixer fitted with the whisk attachment, beat the egg yolks and sugar on high speed until thick and pale in color, about 5 minutes. Slowly mix in 1½ tablespoons of the Kahlúa. Add the mascarpone and whip until just incorporated.

2. In a separate bowl, combine the espresso and remaining ¼ cup Kahlúa. Soak 1 ladyfinger at a time in the espresso mixture and arrange them close together in neat rows in an 8 × 10-inch pan or trifle dish, continuing until the bottom of the pan is completely covered. Pour one-third of the mascarpone mixture over the ladyfingers and smooth the top with a rubber spatula. Repeat to make two additional layers. Dust the top with the cocoa powder, cover, and refrigerate for at least 8 hours before serving.

NOTE My recipe contains raw eggs, so make sure to use the freshest eggs you can find. If you are pregnant, young, elderly, or immunocompromised, you may want to use pasteurized eggs, such as Davidson's Safest Choice pasteurized eggs.

Pineapple Upside-Down Cake

This was one of *the* cakes of my childhood. My mother used a yellow cake mix from a box, canned pineapple, and maraschino cherries from a jar. Even though my version is a bit more upscale and "natural" tasting than my childhood version, it always reminds me of my mom and a simpler time.

Makes one 10-inch cake

PINEAPPLE CARAMEL

¾ cup **sugar**

½ **vanilla bean**, split lengthwise

1 small whole **pineapple**, peeled and cored; quarter and cut one half into ¼-inch thick slices, then coarsely chop the other half

1 cup **heavy cream**

¼ teaspoon **fine sea salt**

Pinch of **ground chile de árbol**

CAKE

1½ cups plus 2 tablespoons **cake flour**

¾ cup fine **yellow cornmeal**

1 teaspoon **baking soda**

¼ teaspoon **baking powder**

¼ teaspoon **fine sea salt**

½ cup **buttermilk**

¼ cup **sour cream**

3 tablespoons **dark rum**

1½ teaspoons **pure vanilla extract**

½ **vanilla bean**, split lengthwise and seeds scraped out

10 tablespoons (1¼ sticks) **unsalted butter**, at room temperature

1¼ cups plus 3 tablespoons **sugar**

3 large **eggs**

1. **Make the pineapple caramel:** Preheat the oven to 350°F. Combine the sugar, vanilla bean, and ½ cup water in a medium saucepan and cook over high heat, without stirring, until it turns into a medium-light caramel, about 6 minutes. Add the chopped pineapple, cream, salt, and chile de árbol and cook until slightly reduced and thickened, about 10 minutes. Remove from the heat and let cool slightly.

2. Working in batches if needed, carefully transfer the mixture to a blender and blend until smooth. Strain through a medium-mesh strainer into a bowl. Return the mixture to the saucepan and cook over high heat, stirring occasionally, until reduced to a saucelike consistency, about 10 minutes. Pour the caramel into a seasoned 10-inch cast-iron skillet and let cool slightly. Arrange the pineapple slices on top of the caramel and set aside.

3. **Make the cake:** Whisk together the flour, cornmeal, baking soda, baking powder, and salt in a medium bowl until combined. Set aside. Whisk together the buttermilk, sour cream, rum, vanilla extract, and vanilla seeds in a measuring cup. Set aside.

4. In the bowl of a stand mixer fitted with the paddle attachment, cream the butter and sugar on high speed until light and fluffy, stopping to scrape down the sides and bottom of the bowl once. Add the eggs one at a time, beating until each is incorporated before adding the next.

5. On medium-high speed, add the flour mixture in three additions, alternating with the buttermilk mixture. Mix until just combined, stopping to scrape down the bowl.

6. Pour the batter into the cast-iron pan on top of the pineapple slices and caramel. Bake until the top is lightly golden brown and a toothpick inserted into the center comes out with a few moist crumbs attached, 30 to 40 minutes. Let cool in the pan on a wire rack for 10 minutes, then invert onto a large platter and let cool for 30 minutes more before serving.

Yogurt Granita with Berry Syrup and Mango

Another great dessert for long, hot summer days after a feast on the grill or a light lunch. Granitas are such an easy dessert to make—just remember to stir everywhere now and then. I love the combination of ripe juicy mangoes and fresh berries, but feel free to choose the fruit combination you prefer. It's even perfect served plain.

Serves 4 to 6

1 quart **full-fat plain Greek yogurt**

2 cups **whole milk**

¼ cup **clover honey**

1 teaspoon **pure vanilla extract**

1 teaspoon finely grated **orange zest**

1 teaspoon finely grated **lemon zest**

Pinch of **kosher salt**

BERRY SYRUP

1 pint fresh **raspberries**

1 pint fresh **blackberries**

1 pint fresh **strawberries**, hulled and halved

½ cup **sugar**

2 teaspoons fresh **lemon juice**

1 tablespoon **raspberry** or blackberry **eau-de-vie**

1 ripe **mango**, pitted, peeled, and finely diced, for serving

1. Whisk together the yogurt, milk, honey, vanilla, orange zest, lemon zest, and salt in a large bowl until smooth. Pour into a baking pan (metal works best). Freeze the mixture until edges begin to set, about 30 minutes.

2. Using a fork, scrape the yogurt mixture to break up the frozen portions. Return the pan to the freezer for 2 to 4 hours more, scraping and breaking up the frozen parts every 20 to 30 minutes, until the mixture resembles fluffy shaved ice.

3. Make the berry syrup: Combine the berries, sugar, and lemon juice in a large bowl and let sit at room temperature for 30 minutes, stirring a few times.

4. Coarsely mash the berries using a potato masher or a fork and pass through a medium-mesh strainer into a bowl, pressing hard on the berries with a rubber spatula to extract as much liquid as possible.

5. Transfer the liquid to a small saucepan and bring to a boil over high heat. Reduce the heat to low and simmer, stirring occasionally, until the mixture is slightly thickened and coats the back of a spoon, about 15 minutes. Stir in the liqueur. Transfer to a bowl, cover, and refrigerate until cold, about 2 hours. The syrup can be made up to 3 days in advance and stored, covered, in the refrigerator.

6. To serve, scrape the granita into serving bowls and drizzle with the syrup. Top with the mango and serve.

No-Bake Chocolate Hazelnut Crema Catalana

At my restaurant Gato in New York City, I serve a more complicated version of this dessert that was created by my amazing pastry chef Clarisa Martino. This is my version, and it's great for a romantic meal for two or any time you need a serious hit of chocolate.

Serves 2

1 cup **half-and-half**

2 ounces **bittersweet chocolate**, coarsely chopped (or use chocolate chips)

2 large **egg yolks**

⅓ cup **sugar**

1 tablespoon **cornstarch**

1 tablespoon **Frangelico**, 1 teaspoon hazelnut syrup, or ¼ teaspoon hazelnut extract

Candied Hazelnuts (recipe follows)

1. Put the half-and-half in a small saucepan and bring to a simmer over high heat. Reduce the heat to low, add the chocolate, and let sit for 1 minute. Whisk until smooth, melted, and well combined.

2. Whisk together the egg yolks, sugar, and cornstarch in a medium bowl until pale and fluffy, about 2 minutes. While whisking continuously, slowly add the hot chocolate mixture to temper the eggs. Return the mixture to the pot and cook, whisking continuously, until thickened, about 2 minutes. Remove from heat and stir in the Frangelico.

3. Set a strainer over a medium bowl. Strain the chocolate custard into the bowl, then divide the custard between two 6-ounce ramekins. Cover the tops with plastic wrap pressed directly against the surface of the custard to prevent a skin from forming. Refrigerate until set, at least 2 hours and up to 24 hours.

4. Top each crema Catalana with some of the candied hazelnuts.

Candied Hazelnuts

Makes about 1 cup

½ cup **sugar**

1 cup whole **hazelnuts**, skins removed

⅛ teaspoon **fine sea salt**

1. Line a baking sheet with parchment paper or a silicone baking mat.

2. Combine the sugar and ¼ cup water in a small saucepan and heat over high heat, swirling, without stirring, until the sugar has dissolved. Bring to a simmer and cook, swirling the pan occasionally, until the mixture turns a medium amber, about 8 minutes. Add the hazelnuts and salt; stir for 1 minute to coat.

3. Pour the mixture onto the prepared baking sheet and immediately separate the nuts using two forks so that each stands alone on the baking sheet. Let cool. Break apart and coarsely chop.

Vanilla Rice Pudding with Rum Raisin Caramel Syrup

I first fell in love with rice pudding as a child when I would order it for dessert at the Greek diner in my neighborhood on the Upper East Side. Comfort food at its best. Using a starchy short-grain rice will yield a creamier version, while baking it in the oven will give your arm a break from the constant stirring that is needed when cooked on the stovetop.

Serves 4 to 6

2 tablespoons **unsalted butter**, softened

¼ cup **Arborio or Carnaroli rice**

4¼ cups **half-and-half**

¼ cup **pure cane sugar**

1 **vanilla bean**, split lengthwise and seeds scraped out

2 **cinnamon sticks**

1 (2-inch) piece **orange zest**

¼ teaspoon **kosher salt**

Rum Raisin Caramel Syrup (recipe follows)

Crème fraîche, for serving (optional)

1. Preheat the oven to 350°F. Butter the bottom and sides of a heavy-duty 3-quart baking dish and put the dish on a baking sheet.

2. Combine the rice, 4 cups half-and-half, the sugar, vanilla bean pod and seeds, cinnamon sticks, orange zest, and salt in the prepared baking dish and mix to combine. Bake for 30 minutes, then remove and stir well, making sure that you are reaching the bottom of the dish. Return to the oven and bake for 15 minutes. Remove and stir well again. Return to the oven and bake until the pudding is creamy and slightly thick and the rice is tender, about 15 minutes longer. Remove and stir in the remaining ¼ cup half-and-half until combined. Discard the cinnamon sticks, vanilla pod, and zest.

3. Serve warm or at room temperature in bowls or goblets, topped with the rum raisin syrup and a touch of crème fraîche, if desired.

Rum Raisin Caramel Syrup

Makes 1 cup

½ cup **golden raisins**

½ cup **dark raisins**

¼ cup plus 2 tablespoons **dark rum**

1 cup **pure cane sugar**

¼ cup **heavy cream**

1 tablespoon **unsalted butter**

1. Bring 2 cups water to a boil in a medium nonreactive saucepan. Remove from the heat and stir in the raisins. Let steep for 30 minutes. Strain the soaking liquid into a small saucepan and add ¼ cup rum. Transfer the raisins to a medium bowl and set aside.

2. Cook the soaking liquid over high heat until reduced to ¾ cup. Add the sugar and cook over medium-high heat, without stirring, until the liquid has evaporated and the sugar has melted and turned a deep amber color, about 8 minutes. Immediately very slowly add the heavy cream (it will bubble up) and the remaining 2 tablespoons rum. Whisk until the mixture is smooth. Whisk in the butter until combined. Add the raisins and transfer the caramel to a heatproof bowl. Let cool at room temperature until warm to the touch.

COCKTAILS

A well-chosen cocktail can set the mood for any gathering in an instant. Hand your guest a chilled martini (see page 221), just a slick of vermouth clouding the icy vodka, and the only thing left to do is turn up the Sinatra: boom—your joint is all class. Plus, can you imagine anyone having a bad time while sipping a Mesa Margarita (page 226)? Pull a pitcher of those out of the fridge, and you're broadcasting that fun times lie ahead. I am an equal-opportunity imbiber, and as long as it's well balanced and never sticky sweet, I can find room in my heart—and bar—for cocktails of all varieties. Leave your car keys at home (thank you, MTA, Lyft, and Uber) and be prepared to Rosé Aperol Spritz (page 230) all day, because at the Flay house, it's summertime and the drinking is easy.

Cocktail Basics

Whether it's a reward for oneself at the end of a long day or a toast with friends to celebrate a good thing to come (or any and everything in between), a well-mixed cocktail can turn a moment into an event. Become the master mixologist of your next gathering, and before you know it, that event will be legendary. I love to get the party started from the get-go and greet my guest at the door with a signature cocktail before switching over to wine at dinner.

I think everyone should know how to make at least one perfect cocktail. Take the challenge and branch out as bartender—remember, your drink starts with a recipe, like anything else. A great cocktail is a matter of knowing the perfect ratios and using high-quality ingredients. You don't need to duplicate the back shelf of your local hangout to make fantastic, creative cocktails, so don't worry about stocking your bar with twelve brands of expensive vodka and a rainbow of brightly colored liqueurs. A half dozen base spirits and a few mixers will allow you to turn out a surprising number of cocktail classics, but also give you enough to tinker with and come up with some cool drinks of your own. (Disclaimer: I do have full bars in all of my homes, but truth be told, I bought very little of the alcohol or equipment myself, because bar stuff makes really great host/hostess gifts. To those of you who stocked my bars, thank you!)

Equipment

The equipment needed to mix a cocktail is easy to acquire, and you don't need a lot of it. The following list should cover every need:

- Bar spoon
- Muddler
- Jigger
- Cocktail shaker
- Strainer
- Ice cube trays

You'll need something to serve those drinks in, too—let's talk glasses! For everyday use in your home bar, you only need six or eight of each of these three basic types: a short glass, a tall glass, and a stemmed glass. If you plan to serve wine at your parties, invest in eight to twelve basic stemmed wineglasses, either in a single shape that is appropriate for both red and white or separate sets of glasses for each.

Essential Liquors

A home bar doesn't have to be a headache: invest in basic equipment and stock up on these essential liquors, and you can have a spread that will impress amateurs—and even make professionals nod in quiet approval.

Gin
Vodka
Bourbon
Whiskey
Scotch whiskey
Vermouth
Orange liqueur
Aperol
Campari
White wine
Red wine
Rosé

Gin

A good-quality gin is a must-have in every bar to make classic martinis, Tom Collinses, and—my personal favorite—a good old gin and tonic. Gin is a neutral spirit enhanced with botanical-based flavorings, the most pronounced one (and the one typically described as "gin-like") being juniper berries.

Classic Gin and Tonic

Serves 1

This highball cocktail is my go-to in the summertime. Light, refreshing, and delicious, an ice-cold G&T never disappoints.

2 **lime wedges**

Ice cubes

3 ounces **gin**

Very cold **tonic water**

Put 1 lime wedge in the bottom of a highball glass and lightly muddle it with a muddler. Fill the glass with ice. Add the gin and fill the glass to the top with tonic (I prefer a ratio of 1½ parts gin to 2 parts tonic); stir a few times to combine. Garnish with the remaining lime wedge and serve.

NOTE For these drinks, my favorites are Hendrick's for the gin and Fever-Tree for the tonic.

Blackberry-Basil Gin and Tonic

Serves 1

An ice-cold, clear gin and tonic is always a welcome sight, but a little color doesn't hurt—this fresh purple iteration of the classic cocktail is as good looking as it is delicious.

3 ripe **blackberries**

1 teaspoon **superfine sugar**

2 teaspoons fresh **lime juice**

1 large fresh **basil leaf**

Ice cubes

3 ounces **gin**

Very cold **tonic water**

1 **lime wedge**

Combine the blackberries, sugar, lime juice, and basil in a highball glass and muddle with a muddler until the blackberries are coarsely mashed. Add the gin and fill the glass to the top with the tonic (I prefer a ratio of 1½ parts gin to 2 parts tonic); stir a few times to combine. Garnish with the lime wedge and serve.

Blackberry-Basil Gin and Tonic

Classic Gin and Tonic

**Dorothy's
Chocolate Martini**

Vodka

The basic building blocks of a martini cocktail are a spirit (gin or vodka) and vermouth, which is a fortified wine flavored with botanicals. The original martini was made with gin, which is why Mr. Bond always specifies a "vodka martini" in his order. Gin and vodka martinis are equally delicious. Vodka is made through the distillation of cereal grains or potatoes that have been fermented, though some modern brands use fruits or sugar. The flavor is clean, neutral, and less botanical than gin.

Vodka Martini

Serves 1

There is something very James Bond about drinking a martini, and whether you like yours shaken or stirred (I like stirred for a gin martini, shaken for vodka), it all starts with the best ingredients. When you have a two-ingredient recipe, there's nothing to hide behind—the ingredients have to be top-notch. With any martini, temperature is also key: you really want these to be icy cold. I always have chilled glasses ready in the freezer in case someone wants a martini. However, if you don't have room, just make sure to freeze your martini glass for at least 10 minutes before making this cocktail.

1 teaspoon **dry vermouth**

Ice cubes

2 ounces **vodka** (my favorite is Ketel One)

Olives, for garnish (optional)

Lemon twist, for garnish (optional)

Pour the vermouth into a chilled martini glass and swirl to coat the inside of the glass. Pour out the excess vermouth. In a shaker full of ice, gently shake or stir the vodka before straining into the glass. Garnish with olives or a lemon twist, if desired, and serve.

Dorothy's Chocolate Martini

Serves 1

This cocktail is dedicated to my mom, Dorothy, who was never seen in Atlantic City without a chocolate martini in her hand. Sweet but never subdued (just like Mom), this martini is a fun one to serve at the end of a dinner party.

2 tablespoons **chocolate syrup**, such as Hershey's

Ice cubes

1 ounce **Godiva dark chocolate liqueur**

1 ounce **Stoli Vanil vodka**

1 ounce **360 Double Chocolate vodka**

1. Spread the chocolate syrup on a small plate and dip the rim of a martini glass in syrup to coat. Place in the freezer while you make the cocktail.

2. Fill a cocktail shaker with ice, add the dark chocolate liqueur, vanilla vodka, and double chocolate vodka, and shake for 10 seconds. Strain the cocktail into the prepared glass and serve.

Bourbon and Whiskey

Whiskey is a spirit distilled from fermented grain mash (corn, barley, wheat, and/or rye), which is then aged in wooden barrels. Made all over the world, it's particularly loved in Ireland and Scotland—and, of course, America. Bourbon is an American-made whiskey that originated in Kentucky, where the lion's share of bourbon producers distill their whiskey. But you don't have to reside in Kentucky, or even the South, to legally make bourbon. The only geographical requisite is that it's made in the United States—any state can produce a whiskey and name it bourbon as long as 51 percent of the grain from which it's distilled is corn and it's aged in new, charred-oak barrels. (Whiskey can be made from any combination of grain, and its oak aging barrels don't need to be new or charred.) Just remember that all bourbon is whiskey, but not all whiskey is bourbon.

Mint Julep

Serves 1

In order to create the best mint julep, start with a good-quality bourbon and don't be stingy with the mint or crushed ice (see Tip).

7 fresh **mint leaves**, plus more for garnish

2 tablespoons **simple syrup** (see Note, page 233)

Crushed ice

3 ounces **bourbon**

In a chilled glass, muddle the mint leaves and the simple syrup. Pack the glass with crushed ice, add the bourbon, then stir vigorously. Add more ice, if necessary. Garnish with mint leaves and serve.

TIP If your refrigerator doesn't have a crushed ice option and your grocery store only sells cubed ice, just fill your food processor halfway with ice cubes and process until finely crushed. Transfer to a large bowl and repeat with more ice. Cover and store in the freezer until you're ready to use.

Whiskey Sour

Serves 1

I feel like the whiskey sour (widely considered to be one of the original whiskey cocktail recipes) is like the gateway cocktail of whiskey drinks. You start drinking whiskey sours, then it's mint juleps, followed by Manhattans, and the next thing you know, you're ordering a couple of fingers of the good stuff, neat. A whiskey sour, then made with bottom-shelf whiskey and bottled sour mix, was definitely one of the first cocktails I ordered when I was sneaking into Manhattan bars in the '80s. My modern version is a bit more upscale and a lot more delicious.

2 ounces **bourbon** (my favorite for mixing is Woodford Reserve)

1 tablespoon fresh **lemon juice**

1 tablespoon **simple syrup** (see Note, page 233), or to taste

Ice cubes

1 **cherry** and/or **orange wedge**, for garnish

Combine the bourbon, lemon juice, and simple syrup in a cocktail shaker. Fill halfway with ice and shake for 10 seconds. Strain into a rocks glass over ice or serve straight up in a martini glass. Garnish with the cherry and/or orange wedge and serve.

Tequila

Tequila is made from blue agave (not cactus) and by law must be made in Mexico. All the brands you know (like Jose Cuervo, Patrón, and others) make five types of tequila: silver, gold, reposado, añejo, and extra añejo, covering the spectrum from young to old, "made for mixing" to "best saved for sipping."

Mesa Margarita

Serves 1

I came up with this margarita in 1991 just before the opening of Mesa Grill New York. That restaurant closed in 2013, but this cocktail still lives on at Mesa Grill Las Vegas and in my home. I like my margaritas relatively dry (and without salt), but if you prefer yours a bit sweeter, just add more simple syrup.

Ice cubes

2 ounces **silver tequila** (my favorite is El Jimador Blanco)

1 ounce **triple sec** or other orange liqueur

1 ounce fresh **lime juice**

¼ teaspoon **simple syrup** (see Note, page 233), or more to taste

1 **lime wedge**, for garnish

1. Fill a cocktail shaker with ice. Add the tequila, triple sec, lime juice, and simple syrup and shake well.

2. *For a margarita on the rocks,* pour the cocktail into a chilled Collins glass filled with ice.

For an up margarita, strain the cocktail into a chilled martini glass.

3. Garnish with the lime wedge and serve.

TIP For serving a crowd, use these basic ratios to stir up a big batch in a pitcher.

Frozen Margarita

Serves 4 to 6

Craving a frozen margarita? There's no need to revert to the acid-green, tequila-spiked slushies of spring breaks gone by. This refreshing, icy cool cocktail has the same proportions of my favorite Mesa margarita, just multiplied to give the blender some traction.

Coarse salt, for rimming the glass (optional)

Lime wedges

8 ounces **silver tequila**

1 cup fresh **lime juice** (from 6 to 8 limes)

4 ounces **triple sec** or other orange liqueur

2 teaspoons **simple syrup** (see Note, page 233), or more to taste

4 cups **ice cubes**

1. For a salt rim, spread some salt over a small saucer. Rub a lime wedge around the rims of glasses and dip the rims into the salt to coat.

2. Combine the tequila, lime juice, triple sec, simple syrup, and ice in a blender and blend until smooth. Pour the mixture into the glasses and garnish with lime wedges.

El Diablo

Serves 1

This is a vintage cocktail from the tequila cocktail collection that features an unexpected combination of crème de cassis, lime, and ginger beer. Here is a great example of a cocktail achieving the balance of flavors that I hold in such high regard: sweet black currant liqueur counters peppery ginger beer, and fresh lime juice brightens golden añejo tequila. It's devilishly good.

1½ ounces **golden añejo tequila**, or you can use a regular reposado

½ ounce **crème de cassis**

½ ounce fresh **lime juice**

Ice cubes

2 to 3 ounces **ginger beer**

1 **lime wedge**

Fresh **blackberry or candied ginger**, for garnish (optional)

In a cocktail shaker, combine the tequila, cassis, lime juice, and 6 ice cubes and shake. Strain into an ice-filled Collins glass and top with the ginger beer. Garnish with the lime wedge and blackberry or ginger, if desired, and serve.

Wine

Wine and Champagne are perfect on their own, especially good ones, so I rarely mess with them—unless I'm in the mood for sangria. It's one of those really easy recipes to put together—you mix it all together, and after a few hours in the fridge, you have the equivalent of adult punch. I like to make red in the cooler months and white in the summer. Sometimes, I also like to create a spritzer by adding a splash of flavored soda water to a crisp white wine, rosé, or light red in the summer, too.

Rosé Aperol Spritz

Serves 8

This cocktail is everything I like in a summer drink: First, it contains rosé. Second, it is not cloyingly sweet. Third, there are bubbles. Altogether, it's the perfect thing to drink on those hot summer days.

1 cup fresh **raspberries**

¾ cup **passion fruit juice**, chilled

¼ cup **Aperol**

¼ cup fresh **lime juice**

2 to 4 tablespoons **simple syrup** (see Note, page 233)

1 (750ml) bottle **sparkling rosé**, chilled

Ruby Red grapefruit wedges, for serving (optional)

1. Spread the raspberries in an even layer on a small baking sheet and freeze for at least 15 minutes and up to 2 hours.

2. Combine the passion fruit juice, Aperol, lime juice, and simple syrup in a pitcher. Add the rosé and raspberries and gently stir to combine. Serve in chilled Champagne flutes with a few frozen raspberries in the bottom of each. Garnish with grapefruit, if desired.

**Summer Fruit
Sangria**

Red Wine Sangria with Fall Fruits and Cinnamon Syrup

Serves 4 to 6

Truth be told, this recipe was created for a guest appearance on Ina Garten's Food Network show a few years ago. Ina and I were testing Thanksgiving recipes, and I was in charge of the cocktail. I have been drinking red wine sangria (and serving it on my restaurant menus) for years. This version really says "fall," with its selection of fruits and simple syrup flavored with cinnamon. Serve it hot, and you have mulled wine.

1 (750ml) bottle **Cabernet Sauvignon**

1½ cups **apple cider**

¼ cup plus 2 tablespoons **apple brandy**

¼ cup plus 2 tablespoons **pear brandy**

½ cup **Cinnamon Simple Syrup** (recipe follows), plus 2 soaked cinnamon sticks (from the simple syrup)

1 small **Gala or Fuji apple**, cored and thinly sliced

1 **Granny Smith apple**, cored and thinly sliced

1 small **red pear**, cored and thinly sliced

1 small **green pear**, cored and thinly sliced

Seeds from 1 small **pomegranate**

½ **orange**, thinly sliced and each slice halved

Ice cubes

Combine the wine, apple cider, apple brandy, pear brandy, simple syrup, and fruits in a large container with a lid or a large pitcher and refrigerate for at least 4 hours and up to 72 hours. Transfer to a pitcher before serving. Serve in red wine goblets over ice.

Cinnamon Simple Syrup

Makes about 1½ cups

1 cup **sugar**

5 **cinnamon sticks**

Combine the sugar and 1 cup water in a small saucepan. Bring to a boil over high heat and cook until the sugar has completely dissolved, about 3 minutes. Transfer the syrup to a container with a lid. Add the cinnamon sticks, cover, and refrigerate for at least 4 hours and up to 48 hours. The longer it sits, the more intense the flavor will be. Remove the cinnamon sticks and save to add to the sangria mixture.

NOTE For regular simple syrup, simply omit the cinnamon sticks.

Summer Fruit Sangria

Serves 4 to 6

Nothing says "summer" (other than a cold glass of rosé) like a large pitcher of white wine sangria, filled to the rim with summer berries and stone fruits. The best part is that you can make it days in advance and chill it in the fridge (which only makes it taste better), so it's always on hand if guests show up for lunch or dinner or just to take a dip in the pool.

1 (750ml) bottle **crisp white wine**, such as Sauvignon Blanc

¼ cup **peach eau-de-vie**

1 cup fresh **orange juice**

2 to 3 cups mixed **fruits** (such as thinly sliced nectarines, peaches, oranges, and/or raspberries)

1 small **lime**, halved and thinly sliced

Ice cubes

Combine the wine, eau-de-vie, orange juice, and fruit in a pitcher and stir to combine. Cover and refrigerate for at least 4 hours and preferably 24 hours before serving. Serve in white wine glasses over ice.

BASICS

The following recipes are not dishes but rather the essential building blocks I use to start and finish my dishes with flavor. A boxed stock may be an adequate substitution for one slow-simmered on the stove, but adequate doesn't always cut it—especially when you want to create a truly well-rounded, full-flavored dish. And sure, there are bottled vinaigrettes galore on the shelves, but nothing will transform a plain bowl of greens or bring a simply grilled piece of fish to life like a drizzle of a bright, fresh vinaigrette you just whisked together. These recipes—stocks, compound butters, pestos, vinaigrettes, and pickled vegetables—are as much about the method as anything else. Endlessly adaptable and easily personalized, these basics are the plain white T-shirts of the cooking world— go ahead and make them your own.

Stocks

Making homemade stock is incredibly easy: You just throw everything into the pot, cover with cold water, and set it on the stove to simmer. A couple of passes with your skimming spoon, a quick strain, and voilà—you have an indispensable tool in your kitchen arsenal. You can season it any way you like, and it freezes beautifully for months. Chicken stock is my go-to, whether it's destined for a bowl of soul-warming chicken noodle soup or serving as a neutral base for endless other soups and sauces. Shrimp stock is another easy one to make ahead and store in your freezer, and unlike the 3 hours needed for chicken stock, this stock only takes 30 minutes. I like using shrimp stock for seafood stews, pastas, and risotto, and it's a must for shrimp and grits. Fish stock is more delicate in flavor and a vital ingredient when making fish dishes where you want to keep the flavor all about the fish and not give it a slight chicken or shrimp flavor.

TIP Save your chicken bones and carcasses when you make a roasted chicken, transfer them to zip-top storage bags, and pop them in the freezer. Do the same for shrimp shells and bones from white fish, if you get them, and you'll be one step closer to homemade stock—whether it's chicken, shrimp, or fish—anytime you want.

Chicken Stock

Makes about 6 cups

Leaving the onion unpeeled adds a golden color to the stock. Just make sure you wash it before cutting.

5 pounds **chicken carcasses**, rinsed well

1 pound **chicken wings**, rinsed well

1 large **Spanish onion**, unpeeled, cut into 1-inch pieces

2 large **carrots**, cut into 1-inch pieces

2 **celery stalks**, cut into 1-inch pieces

8 sprigs **flat-leaf parsley**

2 teaspoons **kosher salt**

1 teaspoon whole **black peppercorns**

1. Combine all the ingredients and 4 quarts cold water in a large stockpot. Bring to a boil; reduce the heat to low and simmer gently, skimming the surface occasionally, until the stock has reduced by one-third, 2½ to 3 hours.

2. Strain the stock through a fine-mesh sieve into a large bowl or a clean pot; discard the solids. Use immediately, or let cool completely, transfer to airtight containers, and store in the refrigerator for up to 3 days or in the freezer for up to 3 months.

Fish Stock

Makes about 8 cups

Saving fish bones in the freezer bound for the stockpot is a great idea, but you need to be picky. Pass on any dark or oily fish like salmon, tuna, or mackerel, as they'll produce a stock with too strong of a fishy flavor.

2 pounds meaty **halibut**, **cod**, or **sea bass bones**, and a **fish head** (if you can get one), split

1 medium **Spanish onion**, thinly sliced

1 **bay leaf**

6 sprigs **flat-leaf parsley**

3 sprigs **thyme**

10 whole **peppercorns**

1 teaspoon **kosher salt**

1. Rinse the fish bones well with cold water. Place the bones in a large stockpot; add the onion, bay leaf, parsley, thyme, peppercorns, salt, and 10 cups cold water. Bring almost to a boil over high heat (do not let it come to a full boil). Reduce the heat to low and cook at a bare simmer, skimming any foam that rises to the surface, until the flavors meld, 20 to 30 minutes.

2. Strain the stock through a fine-mesh sieve lined with cheesecloth into a large bowl or a clean pot; discard the solids. Use immediately, or let cool completely, transfer to airtight containers, and store in the refrigerator for up to 3 days or in the freezer for up to 3 months.

Shrimp Stock

Makes about 8 cups

Find yourself in need of shrimp stock but didn't get to prep it ahead? Try your local fishmonger; they will often have good-quality premade shrimp and lobster stocks available to purchase.

2 tablespoons **canola oil**

5 cups packed **raw shrimp shells, heads, and tails** (about 2 pounds), rinsed well

1 medium **yellow onion**, coarsely chopped

1 small **carrot**, coarsely chopped

1 medium **celery stalk**, coarsely chopped

1 cup **white wine**

2 **plum tomatoes**, coarsely chopped

1 **bay leaf**

10 sprigs **flat-leaf parsley**

½ teaspoon whole **black peppercorns**

1. In a large saucepan, heat the oil over high heat until almost smoking. Add the shrimp shells and tails, onion, carrot, and celery and sauté, stirring occasionally, until the vegetables are soft and the shells turn a deep pink color, about 5 minutes. Add the wine and cook until reduced by half. Add the tomatoes, bay leaf, parsley, peppercorns, and 10 cups cold water. Bring to a boil, then reduce the heat to medium-low. Simmer, skimming the surface occasionally, for 40 minutes.

2. Strain the stock through a fine-mesh sieve lined with cheesecloth into a large bowl or a clean pot, pressing on the solids to extract as much liquid as possible; discard the solids. Use immediately, or let cool completely, transfer to airtight containers, and store in the refrigerator for up to 2 days or in the freezer for up to 3 months.

Vinaigrettes

A well-stocked pantry should always have a variety of vinegars and oils, because there is nothing better than homemade vinaigrette on a freshly made salad. The ratio for a classic French vinaigrette is 3 parts oil to 1 part vinegar, but I prefer mine a bit more acidic, so I do 2 parts oil to 1 part vinegar. Feel free to adjust the given ratios according to your own preference.

I also prefer blended oil (equal parts canola and extra-virgin olive oil) because I find olive oil is usually too assertive when used on its own, while canola is not flavorful enough. You can buy blended oil in grocery stores or just measure out equal quantities of each oil or feel free to adjust the given ratios according to your own preference.

Use the vinaigrettes as you like: classic red or white vinegar is great with simple green salads or grilled vegetable salads; sherry vinaigrette can be drizzled over grilled seafood and pork; and cider vinaigrette is perfect for a fall salad with apples and pears.

Basic Vinaigrette

Makes about ¾ cup

¼ cup **vinegar** of your choosing (red or white wine, aged sherry, cider)

¼ teaspoon **kosher salt**

⅛ teaspoon **freshly ground black pepper**

½ cup **blended oil** (equal parts canola and extra-virgin olive oil)

Whisk together the vinegar, salt, and pepper in a medium bowl until the salt has dissolved. While whisking, slowly drizzle in the oil and whisk until emulsified. Use immediately, or store in an airtight container in the refrigerator for up to 3 days.

Mustard Vinaigrette

Makes about ¾ cup

¼ cup **vinegar** of your choosing (red or white wine, aged sherry, cider)

¼ teaspoon **kosher salt**

⅛ teaspoon **freshly ground black pepper**

1 heaping tablespoon **Dijon mustard**

2 teaspoons finely diced **shallot**

½ cup **blended oil** (equal parts canola and extra-virgin olive oil)

Whisk together the vinegar, salt, pepper, mustard, and shallot in a medium bowl until the salt has dissolved. While whisking, slowly drizzle in the oil and whisk until emulsified. Use immediately, or store in an airtight container in the refrigerator for up to 3 days.

Variation

Fresh Herb Vinaigrette Add 2 teaspoons of your favorite finely chopped fresh herb to any of these vinaigrettes for additional flavor. Fine herbs such as basil, cilantro, parsley, and tarragon work especially well. This variation is particularly good drizzled over poultry or fish.

Citronette

Makes about ¾ cup

In the simplest of translations, a citronette is a vinaigrette made with fresh citrus juice instead of vinegar. Always use the zest of citrus fruits, too—that's where all the flavor and essential oils live.

1 teaspoon finely grated **citrus zest** (such as grapefruit, lemon, lime, orange, or a combination)

¼ cup fresh **citrus juice** (such as grapefruit, lemon, lime, orange, or a combination)

½ teaspoon **kosher salt**

¼ teaspoon **freshly ground black pepper**

1 teaspoon **clover honey** or sugar

½ teaspoon **Dijon mustard**

½ cup **blended oil** (equal parts canola and extra-virgin olive oil)

Whisk together the citrus zest, citrus juice, salt, pepper, honey, and mustard in a medium bowl. While whisking, slowly drizzle in the oil and whisk until emulsified. Use immediately, or store in an airtight container in the refrigerator for up to 3 days.

TIP Salt dissolves more easily in vinegar than in oil, so always add it to the vinegar and let it dissolve before adding the oil.

Pestos

I use pesto for lots of things—it's a fast way to add another dimension of flavor and color to a dish, and it's great when you have lots of herbs hanging out in your refrigerator. Pesto freezes really well, so any time you need a quick sauce for a pasta, an herbaceous lift to a sauce, or a topping for pizza or crostini, it will be there. The most classic pesto is made with fresh basil, pine nuts, and Parmigiano Reggiano, but if you allow yourself to think about pesto as a loose formula rather than a strict recipe, the sky's the limit. A mix of fresh herbs can be used (I like mint and parsley, cilantro and parsley, or sage and parsley), as can any grated dry cheese (I tend to use Parmigiano and Pecorino Romano). Pine nuts are extremely expensive these days, so substituting blanched almonds, pistachios, or hazelnuts is another tasty option.

Here is the classic recipe plus some of my favorite variations. Stick with this basic formula, and you'll never go wrong.

Master Pesto Formula

8 parts **herbs** and/or vegetables	+	2 parts **cheese**	+	2 parts **oil**	+	1 part **nuts**	+	1 to 3 **garlic cloves**
(basil, cilantro, mint, parsley, sage, green onions, fresh green chiles, roasted peppers, tomatoes)		(Parmigiano Reggiano, Pecorino Romano, Manchego, ricotta salata, Asiago, cotija)		(extra-virgin olive oil or something mild such as avocado oil) for a thicker pesto, a bit more for a looser pesto		(pine nuts, almonds, cashews, pistachios, peanuts, hazelnuts)		(the garlic is used raw and it *is* strong, so the amount is up to you)

Classic Pesto

Makes about 1¼ cups

1 **garlic clove**

2 cups packed fresh **basil leaves**

¼ cup **pine nuts**

½ cup **extra-virgin olive oil**

½ cup finely grated **Parmigiano Reggiano cheese**

¼ teaspoon **kosher salt**

¼ teaspoon **freshly grated black pepper**

Put the garlic in a food processor and pulse a few times to chop. Add the basil, pine nuts, and oil and process until smooth. Add the cheese, salt, and pepper and pulse a few times to incorporate. Transfer to a bowl. Use immediately, or transfer to an airtight container and store in the refrigerator for up to 3 days or in the freezer for up to 1 month.

Scallion Pesto

Makes about 1¼ cups

I use this one a lot with fish, and when I do, I leave out the cheese.

1 **garlic clove**

1 cup chopped **scallions**

1 cup packed fresh **flat-leaf parsley**

¼ cup **pine nuts**

½ cup **extra-virgin olive oil**

½ cup finely grated **Parmigiano Reggiano cheese**

¼ teaspoon **kosher salt**

¼ teaspoon **freshly grated black pepper**

Put the garlic in a food processor and pulse a few times to chop. Add the scallions, parsley, pine nuts, and oil and process until smooth. Add the cheese, salt, and pepper and pulse a few times to incorporate. Transfer to a bowl. Use immediately, or transfer to an airtight container and store in the refrigerator for up to 3 days or in the freezer for up to 1 month.

Compound Butters

Compound butters are something I learned to make when I was a student at the French Culinary Institute. Those days may seem like a lifetime ago, but I still find myself falling back on the basic techniques and classic tricks I picked up while I was there. These flavored and blended butters are a simple way to add lots of flavor and a touch of richness to simply prepared foods such as vegetables, grilled meats, steamed fish, and pasta. I always have several flavors in my freezer to use any time I need them. To freeze the butter for future use, I scrape it onto a piece of parchment paper and roll it tightly into a log, then store the roll in the freezer in a zip-top plastic storage bag to prevent odors and freezer burn.

Harissa-Mint Butter

Makes about 1½ cups

I particularly like using this North African–inspired flavored butter to finish chicken, lamb, or pork dishes and to top meaty fish such as swordfish and halibut.

1 cup (2 sticks) **unsalted butter**, softened

½ cup **harissa**

¼ cup packed fresh **mint leaves**, chopped

1 teaspoon **kosher salt**

Combine the butter, harissa, mint, and salt in a food processor and process until smooth. Scrape the butter into a 16-ounce ramekin. Press a circle of parchment paper directly on top of the butter, then wrap the ramekin in foil. Refrigerate for at least 1 hour and up to 3 days before using.

Anchovy Butter

Makes about 1¼ cups

One summer when I was in Rome, I had a simple dish of bucatini with anchovy butter and Parmigiano Reggiano. As simple as it was, each bite was so mouthwateringly flavorful that I would rank it among the best dishes I have ever eaten. So yes, put this on pasta, but it's also phenomenal for adding a hit of super-savory, garlicky flavor to grilled seafood or fish or even steak.

1 cup (2 sticks) **unsalted butter**, softened

5 **garlic cloves**, finely chopped and mashed to a paste with the side of a chef's knife and ¼ teaspoon of kosher salt

16 **anchovies packed in oil**, drained, patted dry, and finely chopped

1 teaspoon fresh **lemon juice**

¼ teaspoon **kosher salt**

¼ teaspoon **coarsely ground black pepper**

Combine the butter, garlic, anchovy, lemon juice, salt, and pepper in a medium bowl and mix until smooth. Scrape the butter into a 16-ounce ramekin. Press a circle of parchment paper directly on top of the butter, then wrap the ramekin in foil. Refrigerate for at least 1 hour and up to 3 days before using.

Cilantro-Chile Butter

Makes about 1½ cups

Fruity, floral, and with just the right amount of heat, Fresno chiles are simply amazing. They pair beautifully with verdant cilantro in this butter, which is superb with grilled lobster, crabs, and chicken.

1 cup (2 sticks) **unsalted butter**, softened

⅓ cup finely chopped fresh **cilantro leaves**

3 **Fresno chiles**, stemmed, seeded, and finely diced

Finely grated **zest of 2 limes**

1 teaspoon **kosher salt**

Combine the butter, cilantro, chiles, lime zest, and salt in a medium bowl and mix until smooth. Scrape the butter into a 16-ounce ramekin. Press a circle of parchment paper directly on top of the butter, then wrap the ramekin in foil. Refrigerate for at least 1 hour and up to 3 days before using.

Pickled
Chiles
(page 249)

Pickled Vegetables

Truth be told, I love just about anything when it's pickled. Pickles are great for munching on on their own, tucking into sandwiches, or adorning a cheese plate. They add a touch of brightness and acidity to any dish.

Basic Pickled Vegetables

Makes almost 5 cups

I kept this basic quick-pickle brine simple so it can be used with virtually any vegetable. For more flavor punch, swap in different vinegars or add additional spices and herbs.

2 cups **vinegar** (cider, distilled white, or red wine vinegar)

½ cup **sugar**

2 tablespoons **kosher salt**

1 tablespoon **whole black peppercorns**

1 tablespoon **coriander seeds**

1½ pounds **vegetables** (carrots, cucumbers, green beans, asparagus), cut to your liking

1. Combine the vinegar, sugar, salt, peppercorns, coriander, and 2 cups cold water in a medium nonreactive saucepan. Bring to a boil over high heat. Reduce the heat to low and simmer for 5 minutes.

2. Pack the vegetables into a heatproof resealable nonreactive container or jar with a lid (divide them among several containers, if necessary). Pour the hot brine over the vegetables. Let cool to room temperature, then cover and chill for at least 2 hours before serving. The vegetables will keep in the refrigerator for up to 1 month.

(recipes continue)

**Pickled
Red Onions
(page 248)**

**Pickled Shrimp
(page 50)**

Pickled Red Onions

Makes about 2 cups

I have a large jar of homemade pickled red onions in my refrigerator at all times. They're the perfect way to add brightness and crunch to a dish, and I love topping pizza, avocado relish, fish tacos, and nachos with them. Honestly, sometimes I just eat them on their own. Grenadine adds an additional touch of sweetness while amplifying the onions' vibrant magenta color.

3 cups **red wine vinegar**

1 cup fresh **lime juice**

½ cup **sugar**

¼ cup **grenadine**

1 tablespoon **kosher salt**

2 large **red onions**, halved and thinly sliced

1. Combine the vinegar, lime juice, sugar, grenadine, salt, and 1 cup water in a large saucepan. Bring to a boil over high heat and cook, whisking a few times, until the sugar has dissolved, about 5 minutes. Remove from the heat and let cool for 5 minutes.

2. Put the onions in a nonreactive container with a lid and pour the brine over the top. Cover and refrigerate for at least 1 hour and up to 48 hours before serving. The onions will keep in the refrigerator for up to 3 months.

Yucatán Pickled Onions

Makes about 1 cup

These pickled onions, flavored with the citrus and allspice central to the cuisine of Mexico's Yucatán Peninsula, are delicious on fish tacos (see page 169), on sandwiches, or in salads.

½ cup fresh **grapefruit juice**

½ cup fresh **orange juice**

½ cup fresh **lime juice**

¼ cup **white wine vinegar**

1 tablespoon **sugar**

1 teaspoon **kosher salt**

½ teaspoon **whole black peppercorns**

½ teaspoon **allspice berries**

1 **bay leaf**

1 large **red onion**, halved and thinly sliced

1. Combine the citrus juices, vinegar, sugar, salt, peppercorns, allspice, bay leaf, and ½ cup water in a medium saucepan. Bring to a boil over high heat and cook, whisking, until the sugar has dissolved, about 2 minutes. Remove from the heat and let cool for 5 minutes.

2. Put the onions in a nonreactive container with a lid and pour the brine over the top. Cover and refrigerate for at least 1 hour and up to 48 hours before serving. The pickles will keep in the refrigerator for up to 3 months.

Pickled Chiles

Makes about 1 cup

The crowning touch to any plate of nachos, these pickled chiles are a thousand times fresher than the canned variety. I am particularly fond of them as a garnish for Brussels Sprout Nachos (page 63) or adding spice to a Mesa Margarita (page 226) and not to mention on a cheeseburger—of the green chile variety (see page 146) or not.

2 cups **red wine vinegar**

3 tablespoons **sugar**

1 teaspoon **kosher salt**

8 large **Fresno chiles** or jalapeños, or 16 serrano chiles, thinly sliced

1. Combine the vinegar, sugar, salt, and ¼ cup water in a small saucepan. Bring to a boil and cook, whisking a few times, until the sugar and salt have dissolved, about 2 minutes. Remove from the heat and let cool for 10 minutes.

2. Put the chiles in a nonreactive container with a lid and pour the brine over the top. Chill for at least 1 hour and up to 48 hours before serving. The chiles will keep in the refrigerator for up to 2 months.

Acknowledgments

Obviously, no one creates an entire cookbook on their own, including me. So, allow me to thank the following people for always showing up and getting it done. A special thank-you to Stephanie and Sally, as always—I really couldn't do this without the two of you.

Stephanie Banyas
Sally Jackson
Elyse Tirrell
Christie Bok
Ed Anderson
Jeanne Lurvey
Hayley Lucaczyk
Pablo Munoz
Renee Forsberg
Gato Restaurant
Dahlia Warner
Courtney Fuglein
Julie Morgan
Dana Zukofsky

Jimmy Ventura
Laurence Kretchmer
Food Network
Irika Slavin
Marysarah Quinn
Ian Dingman
Kate Tyler
Stephanie Davis
Joyce Wong
Kim Tyner
Bullfrog & Baum
Yosmar Brito
Cumanda Rivadeneira
Julie McCrary

Kalamazoo Grills
Laura Sommers
KitchenAid
Mandy Ruholl-Cook
Boos Board
Adèle Schober
Breville

And last, but certainly not least, my editor, Jennifer Sit

Index

Dorothy and Bobby
November 1972

Published in the United States by Clarkson Potter/
Publishers, an imprint of Random House, a division of
Penguin Random House LLC, New York.
clarksonpotter.com

CLARKSON POTTER is a trademark and POTTER with
colophon is a registered trademark of Penguin Random
House LLC.

Library of Congress Cataloging-in-Publication Data
Names: Flay, Bobby, author.
Title: Bobby at home : Fearless Flavors from My Kitchen/
 Bobby Flay with Stephanie Banyas and Sally Jackson.
Description: First edition. | New York : Clarkson Potter,
 [2019] | Includes index.
Identifiers: LCCN 2018052578| ISBN 9780385345910
 (hardcover) | ISBN 9780385345927 (ebook)
Subjects: LCSH: Cooking. | LCGFT: Cookbooks.
Classification: LCC TX714 .F628 2019 | DDC 641.5--dc23
LC record available at https://lccn.loc.gov/2018052578

ISBN 978-0-385-34591-0
Ebook ISBN 978-0-385-34592-7

Printed in China

Book and cover design by Ian Dingman

10 9 8 7 6 5 4 3 2 1

First Edition

Also by Bobby Flay

Bobby Flay Fit
Brunch @ Bobby's
Bobby Flay's Barbecue Addiction
Bobby Flay's Bar Americain Cookbook
Bobby Flay's Throwdown!
Bobby Flay's Burgers, Fries & Shakes
Bobby Flay's Grill It!
Bobby Flay's Mesa Grill Cookbook
Bobby Flay's Grilling for Life
Bobby Flay's Boy Gets Grill
Bobby Flay Cooks American
Bobby Flay's Boy Meets Grill
Bobby Flay's From My Kitchen to Your Table
Bobby Flay's Bold American Food